D. Caroline Coile, Ph.D.

Greyhounds

Everything About Purchase, Care,
Nutrition, Behavior, and Training

Filled with Full-color Photographs

Illustrations by Tana Hakanson and
Michele Earle-Bridges

CONTENTS

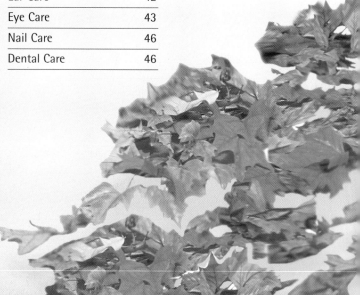

IN THE COURSE OF TIME

Unleashed, her flight begins. Soaring in leaps and bounds, she outstrips the wind, until, with sides heaving she returns to her master, who too has soared through the eyes of the Greyhound. No matter that the quarry was not caught, or indeed, that there was anything but the horizon to chase—sharing this quiet time, punctuated only by the cadence of pounding feet, is what binds Greyhound and human. It has been thus throughout the ages.

The Ancient Greyhound

In the year 124 A.D., the Greek historian Arrian wrote of hunting with Greyhounds:

"The true sportsman does not take out his dogs to destroy the Hares, but for the sake of the course, and the contest between the dogs and the Hares, and is glad if the Hare escapes."

Yet the Greyhound's roots reach even further into antiquity, to a time when the human unleashed the dog not for sport, but to provide meat for sustenance. The wide expanses of North Africa and Arabia provided a land where speed reigned. A dog that could overtake fleeing game and bring it back to share with its human pack members was a valuable animal, and the discriminating breeding of such animals tended to reproduce fleetness. Thus, one of the first specialized types of dogs to be selectively bred was the Greyhound. Since time immemorial it has been one of the most consistently bred and revered forms of domesticated animals.

His ancestors were celebrated by pharaohs, poachers, and paupers alike.

Dogs of undeniable Greyhound form were depicted on the tombs of ancient Pharaohs over 4,000 years ago. The beauty of the Greyhound, one of four things "comely in going" (according to some translations from the Hebrew), was recorded by Solomon in Proverbs (30: 29-31). Yet the ancient Greyhound was not the Greyhound as we know it today.

Dogs of the Pharaohs were more like the Saluki, a Middle-Eastern Greyhoundlike breed. The Saluki was a dog of the nomad, and as such would have traveled throughout the desert lands. Although it was so revered that it was never sold, it was on occasion presented as a gift to an esteemed visitor. No doubt Salukis—also called Persian Greyhounds—were presented to the caravan traders, and through them were introduced even farther throughout the world. The desert Greyhounds eventually found themselves in Babylon, Afghanistan, Russia, Turkistan, Greece, Rome, Gaul, and Britain. Different subtypes developed to adapt to the various climates, terrain, and game in these different locales. The Greyhounds of the colder climates were crossed with other native breeds to achieve thicker coats. Thus there came to be a family of related dogs having in common a sleek build and the ability to hunt game by sight, a family now known as the sighthounds. The quintessential sighthound is the Greyhound.

Through the Ages

The sighthounds of Greece, Rome, and later, Britain seemed to most resemble the modern Greyhound, and today's Greyhound descends mostly from the British form. By Saxon times Greyhounds were well established in Britain and were valued both by commoners for their ability to feed the family and by nobility for the sport of the chase.

Forest Laws

The year 1014 marked the beginning of an ignoble four-century chapter in Greyhound history: the enactment of the Forest Laws. Serfs and slaves were prohibited from Greyhound ownership, and Greyhounds owned by freemen living near the royal forests had to be lamed, either by chopping three toes off a front paw or by severing ligaments in the knee. This mutilation was to prevent a commoner from attempting to hunt game for food at the expense of royal sport.

Coursing

Even after the Forest Laws were repealed, Greyhounds remained dogs of the nobility. With the growing importance of agriculture and domestic animals for food, the reliance of commoners on Greyhounds for sustenance had been greatly reduced. Coursing—the pursuit of game by sighthounds—was increasingly for sport among both nobles and commoners. Elizabeth I, a coursing enthusiast, decreed that rules be set forth by which dogs could be fairly judged, thus setting the stage for the "sport of queens." In 1776 the first coursing club was formed, and during the 1800s coursing became an important pastime for the upper class.

In the late 1700s Lord Orford, an enthusiastic if eccentric coursing devotee, set about to improve Greyhounds by crossing them with other breeds. One of the least likely crosses had to be that with the Bulldog, which at that time resembled more the Pit Bull of today. Amid the contempt and ridicule of his competitors,

Greyhound-like dogs, such as these from the Egyptian tomb of Rekh-me-Re (ca. 1450 B.C.) are among the earliest recognizable domesticated canines.

Built for Speed

Greyhounds are fast for many reasons. These involve the breed's unique physiology, including an unusually large and strong heart, blood that is extra rich in oxygen-carrying red blood cells, low body fat percentage, and high percentage of fast-twitch muscle fibers. Other reasons involve the Greyhound's structure, with long legs and supple, slightly arched back. These features enable it to run in a style known as the double-suspension gallop. When most dogs gallop, they are totally suspended in air only when all four feet are contracted under the body. Some dogs, most notably Greyhounds and their relatives, have a second phase of suspension, which occurs

The Greyhound's double-suspension gallop is more typically cat-like than dog- or horse-like in form. There are two periods when all four feet are off the ground (seen in the rightmost figure of each line).

when all the legs are fully extended in front and behind the body. This enables them to run in leaps, adding speed but at the expense of stamina.

Lord Orford bred this cross back to Greyhounds for seven generations. Then, to the further shock of his competitors, he took his best crossbreed to the coursing field and promptly won every course. Simply put, the hybrid Czarina could not be beaten. Still Lord Orford's fellow coursing enthusiasts refused to touch the Bulldog blood. Only after Czarina's grandsons, Snowball and Major, proved themselves to be similarly invincible was the new blood accepted. It can be said that every present-day Greyhound traces back to these two dogs.

Coming to America

Greyhounds had also made their way to America, having accompanied the Spanish in their expeditions of the early 1500s. It was not uncommon for early European explorers to include a Greyhound among the dogs that accompanied them across country, and a

Greyhound was even a well-known figure at Valley Forge during the Revolutionary War. But only when the settlers began to farm the Midwest did the Greyhound arrive en masse. As crops were overrun with jackrabbits, European immigrants naturally recalled the coursing prowess of Greyhounds and had them brought from Europe for vermin control. Again, sport grew from necessity, and the coursing of jackrabbits, coyotes, and other game on the plains became a popular pastime. General Custer was known to keep a large number of Greyhounds, and Teddy Roosevelt also enjoyed hunting with Greyhounds.

Two Halves of One Breed

The problem with coursing as a sport was that it was not readily accessible to the masses. Closed-park coursing, in which the dogs were let loose after a rabbit in an enclosed area,

attracted great public attention in England for a while, but soon lost favor. In 1876 the first exhibition of Greyhounds chasing a mechanical rabbit was held in England, but was viewed only as a curiosity. It failed, too, in the United States, where it was presented as a side event to horse racing. It was not until the Greyhound races were staged at night under artificial lighting that they erupted as an entertainment spectacle. Track racing quickly outpaced coursing in popularity, both in Europe and America.

In racing, the emphasis is upon speed, with little attention to the agility and endurance required of a coursing dog. The coursing dogs provided the stock from which the racing dogs were developed, but soon the racing dogs were bred only with each other. In America racing Greyhounds are registered with the National Greyhound Association (NGA). The coursing dogs also provided the foundation for another modern type of Greyhound: the show Greyhound.

At the turn of the nineteenth century the exhibition of purebred dogs was beginning to catch the sporting interest of many, and Greyhounds were among the earliest breeds to be exhibited. Ideally, a dog that was built right would run right, although many of the best coursing dogs were admittedly lacking in looks. Most of the early show winners were prominent coursing dogs, but as judges came to favor dogs with fewer rough edges, those with a layer of fat tended to win out. The sinewy coursing dogs lost and returned to the field, and show Greyhounds began to be bred to each other. In the United States these dogs were the foundation stock for today's American Kennel Club (AKC)–registered Greyhounds.

Which is the true Greyhound? Both the NGA and AKC Greyhounds have an equal right to lay claim to the title of Greyhound. They came initially from the same stock, but represent the results of selection with different priorities. Still, the Greyhound of today is nonetheless remarkably unchanged from the Greyhound of 1,000 years ago.

In many breeds of dogs the goal of the breeder is to change and thus improve the breed. Greyhound breeders have the challenge of preserving this ancient breed, already perfected by thousands of generations of selection. This challenge has fallen to the breeders of the show-type Greyhound, and the best of them are striving to produce Greyhounds that are athletic, intelligent, healthy, and beautiful, with the look and coursing ability of the Greyhound of antiquity.

The Whippet (left) is a smaller version of the Greyhound.

The AKC Versus the NGA Greyhound

What a choice—do you want a svelte and loving AKC Greyhound, or a svelte and loving NGA Greyhound? Although both strains are clearly Greyhounds, AKC Greyhounds tend to be taller but narrower, with deeper chests, longer necks and legs, more arched backs, more angulated rear legs, longer, lower tails, and smaller, more tightly folded ears—in short, everything thought of as "Greyhound" is essentially accentuated. They are more successful in conformation shows.

NGA Greyhounds are longer and wider-bodied, with thicker tails and bunchier muscles. Their fur may be less sleek, they have a greater tendency to have missing thigh hair, and the self-colors (no spots) predominate. NGA Greyhounds have a tendency to be keener for the chase, and are undeniably faster than AKC Greyhounds. Because of this they also are more likely to run to the point of hurting themselves. NGA Greyhounds tend to be more successful at lure-coursing.

Probably the main consideration between an NGA or AKC Greyhound is whether or not you must have a puppy. Most NGA Greyhounds become available only after they have finished their racing careers. Some may be yearlings that were either injured or didn't make the grade, but most are between two and four years of age. With a life expectancy of 10 to 14 years, this still gives you plenty of time. Having been raised in a kennel, home life will be totally foreign to these dogs. They may or may not be

Rescue organizations have made family pets out of thousands of retired racers.

trustworthy with other pets. They do adjust to home life with incredible speed, however. In fact, these dogs combine the best of puppies and adults, in that you still have all the enjoyment of showing them the world, yet they are

a lot smarter than puppies! It is undeniably very special to save the life of a retired racer, but keep in mind that the AKC Greyhound puppy could need you just as much.

Running into Problems

For a breed that has been so idolized throughout its long history, the Greyhound has seen its share of hard times. But perhaps at no time has the Greyhound's future been so tenuous as now. The Greyhound is one of the most populous breeds in this country, with more than 30,000 born annually. Its sleek silhouette has long made it a favorite emblem and model for advertising. Everybody knows the Greyhound. Yet the AKC ranks the Greyhound as one of the least popular of the breeds it recognizes, with fewer than 200 registered annually. And until recently, the sight of a pet Greyhound was a rarity.

Why the lack of popularity for the Greyhound as pet? Many people have wrongly assumed that Greyhounds are not interested in being pets, that all they want to do is run, that they are hyperactive, aggressive, unloving, and unavailable. In fact, those Greyhounds that have found their ways into homes are proving those assumptions to be dead wrong. Today, many families have discovered that Greyhounds make even better pets than they did race dogs, and the adoption of ex-racers has reached unprecedented numbers (see following chapter).

This popularity has come at the expense of the show Greyhound, however. Responsible breeders do not breed a litter unless there are homes lined up for puppies, and the greater availability of retired racers has meant that most people wanting a pet Greyhound get a Greyhound from racing stock, not show stock. There is further con-

cern among show breeders that because the track dogs have not been bred for health or longevity, they bring with them a bevy of hereditary problems previously unheard of in the breed.

Although the majority of adoptees are neutered, some remain intact and could be registered with the AKC. If these dogs were bred, show breeders fear that the influx of their genes into the AKC Greyhound gene pool could swamp the AKC show Greyhound type. Some breeders argue that NGA dogs may introduce hereditary health problems to the AKC pool, but others contend that the NGA dogs provide a reservoir that AKC breeders can tap if hereditary health problems ever became problematic in their small gene pool.

Whether NGA, AKC, or something in between, everyone agrees the Greyhound makes a beautiful and loving companion.

The Greyhound as a Pet

Dog breeds differ as much in actions as in appearances. The Greyhound is every bit as specialized in behavior as it is in form. Hounds differ from other hunting breeds in that they must act independently—a Greyhound that paused to check back with its master while chasing a hare would be a very poor coursing dog. Greyhounds were bred to chase without question or human direction; they will be happy to chase cats and run amok around the neighborhood, with or without your approval. Under no circumstances can a Greyhound be trusted to stay in your yard without a leash or fence. A blowing bit of paper or squirrel seen across the street can spell disaster.

Traits

✔ Most people are very surprised to discover how easy the Greyhound is to live with. Another trait of the coursing dog as compared to other hunting dogs is that the coursing dog is bred for a quick burst of energy. Its job is over in minutes. Thus, like the cheetah, the Greyhound tends to sleep for a large part of the day, conserving its energy for use in an explosive burst. Still, the Greyhound needs the daily opportunity to burn that energy it has so carefully stored throughout the day.

✔ Greyhounds can be good apartment dogs, as long as their owner is absolutely committed to a regular exercise regime for the dog. They sleep a lot and are accustomed to relieving themselves during scheduled outings, but again, they can never be let out unsupervised. Ex-racers are used to routine, and do not understand the concept of "in just a minute."

✔ Greyhounds have been selected to hunt and live together without fighting. A Greyhound will occasionally get into an argument with another dog, but will generally not look for trouble, as the flight instinct is stronger than the fight instinct. Greyhounds live together well.

✔ Greyhounds are extremely tolerant dogs, but they don't have the padding to protect them from rough children. Their lack of eagerness for constant play may make them frustrating for some children. And beware that wagging whip-like Greyhound tail—ouch!

✔ Greyhounds are a "soft" breed and must be treated and trained gently. They learn quickly, but they become bored easily. They often respond to obedience commands with the speed of a tired slug.

✔ Greyhounds are used to doing as they're told, and are not a breed that will engage in dominance disputes. Although not as demonstrative as many breeds, the Greyhound takes its commitment to family seriously and may not take easily to transferring to new homes once the attachment has been made.

✔ Greyhounds are not eager barkers, and make poor watchdogs. They are not biters.

✔ Many people compare the Greyhound to a cat—independent, somewhat aloof, and very conscious of creature comforts. They love to be stroked and many will even rub against you in a catlike manner. Theirs is a quiet, dignified affection, more likely conveyed by resting their head in your lap than by licking or fawning. It is possible to train a Greyhound to stay off the furniture, but in all fairness you should supply a soft, preferably raised, bed of its own. The Greyhound does not have built-in padding, and in fact it is prone to callous and bursa formation if deprived of soft bedding. Nor does it have built-in insulation, so it should be protected from extremes in temperature.

✔ Greyhounds are by no means small dogs, with NGA males averaging from 65 to 85 pounds (29–39 kg), and NGA females from 50 to 65 pounds (23–29 kg). They will greet you by jumping up on you, and could inadvertently knock down a frail or unsuspecting person. Greyhounds can also scout your kitchen counters for tasty morsels and steal them with lightning speed. They do not believe in sleeping curled in a ball, but seem to prefer to stretch to their limits in order to take up as much room as possible—especially if sharing your bed.

✔ The Greyhound's coat is wash and wear. They shed, as do all dogs, but have little doggy odor.

✔ The Greyhound's quest for speed makes it more prone to injuries and lameness than other breeds. The breed has no fear of approaching cars and will seldom move out of the way.

Remember: A good fence, ready leash, soft bed, gentle touch, and warm heart are all necessities for Greyhound ownership.

SAVING GREYS

Eight Greyhounds parade under the floodlights, their quivering muscles the only clue to their excitement. As the lure begins its journey, the Greyhounds howl their frustration at being confined in the starting box, until finally the doors spring open and the dogs bound forward. Their sprint around the track defines single-minded determination, oblivious to the crowd, each other, and even their own injuries. At the end of the race, the eighth-place finisher is as pleased with himself as is the first-place finisher. Unfortunately, his trainer is not.

The trainer has reason to be unhappy if a Greyhound runs poorly. The trip around the track is the culmination of a very long and costly journey that began long before that dog was born. It began with the choice of the best possible brood bitch and a substantial stud fee, and continued with optimal prenatal and postnatal care, socialization, handling, and schooling. By the time a pup enters his first race, several thousand dollars have already been invested in him. And he has yet to earn a penny back.

Life on the Farm

Most pups begin life inside a nursery room with their dam and littermates; the average litter size is about seven. After weaning, the litter moves to larger quarters, usually a long run with access to an indoor enclosure.

Retired racers thrive in the lap of luxury— or any lap!

Early lure training starts as a game, with the pups falling over each other to catch a dragged toy. As they get keener for the game, they begin to chase and jump in their efforts to snatch the prize.

Some Greyhound litters will be sent to a rearing facility at four months of age. By this age the dogs should have received abundant handling and can usually walk on a leash. The pups are put in small groups in a larger paddock so that they can run and cavort with their littermates, building strength and coordination. They may also be allowed access to a large field for unlimited running. At 10 to 12 months of age, the Greyhound may once again change homes to live at a training facility. Here his formal education starts, beginning with a change to living in a small kennel, or a cage. The track Greyhound's life is one of routine. The day begins early with the first of three to four paddock "turnouts" of the day. While together, each dog wears a kennel muzzle to protect each other from overzealous play or squabbles with other dogs.

The Inside Track

Many people assume that Greyhounds must be trained to chase live rabbits in order to build some sort of blood lust for the chase. But 2,000 years of breeding have resulted in a dog that is just looking for an excuse to chase something, and this instinct does not need priming with live prey. On the track the dog chases a lure, not a rabbit, and serious training is aimed at encouraging enthusiasm for the lure only. In many states it is illegal for dogs to be trained to chase live animals, but some trainers still believe that they can get an edge by training with live rabbits. Those unethical trainers who are caught doing this are barred from further NGA competition.

Lure enthusiasm is built by tempting the pups with a pole lure (see page 66) outside of their runs. Yearlings are allowed to chase a lure as it is pulled at high speed in a long straight line by a motorized device called a *jack-o-lure*; once they are good at that they practice making high-speed turns by chasing a lure moving in a small circle with a device called a *whirly-gig*. The next step is introduction to the schooling track, where the trainees get their first look at a real track lure and will eventually learn to break from a starting box and run with other dogs.

Win, Place, Show . . . or Go

Yet another change of home may occur when the Greyhound goes to the racing kennel, which usually houses about 60 dogs. A dog will spend the season at the same track, but may change tracks the next season. Each Greyhound

Amazing Greys

✔ In a sport where speed rules, the record-setting kings and queens are Be My Bubba, who ran 5/16 of a mile in 29.33 seconds, DC's Dunkit, who ran 3/8 of a mile in 36.30 seconds, and Runaround Sue, who ran 7/16 of a mile in 42.57 seconds.

✔ JR's Ripper won a record-setting 143 races in his career, but the all-time money earner is Be My Bubba, with $318,000 so far.

✔ "Most stamina" award goes to Mi Top Hand, who ran in 367 races, but "most determined" would have to go to Jamies Simoneyes, who ran in 170 races—without a single win.

✔ The most ever paid for a greyhound was $500,000 for P's Rambling.

may race every three to seven days. Dogs start at the bottom, proving themselves against other novice Greyhounds. When they win a race, they move up to compete in a tougher class. Only a few will ever get to race in Class A; only the best will ever win in it. After a number of losses, depending on class, they move down to a lower class. When they eventually can't win even in Class D, or when they have an injury that will render them noncompetitive, their racing days are over.

Those dogs that have had illustrious careers may still have a future as a breeding animal, but most do not. This is where Greyhound adoption comes in to play.

Fate of the Retired Racer

The American Greyhound Council (AGC) was formed in the 1980s in part to advance the welfare of racing Greyhounds. By promoting the adoption of retirees, underwriting many of the expenses, and encouraging a reduction in breeding, a milestone was reached in 1994: For the first time, more Greyhounds were adopted (about 14,000) than were euthanized (about 13,000). Unless a dog is severely injured or has a personality problem, at most good tracks every retiree has a chance at adoption. In addition, AGC-sponsored research into improved track design has greatly reduced the number of injuries that often bring a dog's racing career to an end.

There is a feeling among some of the public that racing Greyhound owners and trainers are satanic beings who regularly abuse the dogs in their care. This perception is fueled by some well-publicized cases of Greyhound kennels full of neglected dogs. The NGA has now implemented a tough surprise inspection program; those failing to make the grade are permanently banned from racing. Nonetheless, with approximately 50 tracks, 2,000 farms, and several hundred trainers in operation, some abuses are bound to slide by undetected.

The truth is that Greyhound people are no different from the rest of humankind. There are both top-notch and unscrupulous people among Greyhound caretakers. The irresponsible Greyhound owners have the chance to maltreat a lot of dogs at once, but they do so at risk of their income and career.

Two major problems are at the root of the dog crisis in the United States: overbreeding and the inability to take lifelong responsibility for a dog. Racing Greyhound breeders are guilty of both. Yet even they have lamented the fact that success in Greyhound racing depends largely upon breeding so many dogs that a few are bound to turn out winners. Breeders realize that everyone involved would be better off if they

could agree to breed fewer dogs, and from 1990 to 1999 they reduced the number of Greyhounds born in the United States from 52,000 to 33,000. About 18,000 Greyhounds are adopted each year; combined with the number that are retired to breeding kennels, this means the percentage of euthanized retirees has dropped to about 20 percent—that's still 20 percent too many.

Greyhound racing is not a lucrative enterprise. In order to make a living by racing dogs, a trainer must know when to cut losses and give up on a dog that cannot earn its keep, and to do this without letting sentiment cloud logic. The rest of the kennel's welfare depends on it. It is simply not possible to make pets of the many dogs in a Greyhound kennel. Keeping a dog in a cage for most of the day is not a preferred way for a pet to live. Having been raised in this manner, however, most of the Greyhounds in a well-run Greyhound kennel are nonetheless well-adjusted to their lifestyle. They wag their tails and greet visitors with the gusto of any dog, but seem content to spend most of their day snoozing. Once given the chance to live the life of a pet, however, they never look back.

TIP

Adoption Contacts

Two good places to find an adoption group are the Greyhound Pets of America web page at *http://www.Greyhoundpets.org/* or by phone at 1-800-366-1472 and The Greyhound Project's web page at *http://www.adopt-a-Greyhound.org/*.

In the past, Greyhounds racing for the finish line were literally running for their lives.

Future racers spend most of their time just being puppies.

Some Greyhounds are stars on the track; others aspire to be stars on the couch.

"Ahhhhh . . . this is more like it!"

Retired racers make fast friends.

"A family all my own?" Greyhounds can make their ears stand at attention when something really interesting comes up. Notice the NGA tattoos in this retired racer's ears.

All dressed up and ready to run. The racing muzzle not only ensures safety, but also makes it easier to determine a winner in a photo finish.

The NGA (racing) Greyhound tends to have a more moderate form, with fewer extreme angles than does the AKC (show) Greyhound.

The AKC (show) Greyhound tends to have a deeper chest, longer neck, more angled rear, and thinner tail than the NGA (racing) Greyhound.

A Heart Racing with Love

Many tracks have their own adoption facilities. In addition, more than 200 Greyhound adoption groups exist in the United States. Some are small independent groups and others are large national organizations. Some have their own kennel facilities, and some place their dogs in foster homes for training while awaiting adoption. Most are run by experienced Greyhound people, but a few are guided more by good intentions than good sense. Reputable groups will screen applicants carefully to make sure they can properly take care of a Greyhound and to arrange the best possible match of dog and family. Don't expect that these dogs will be free or even cheap. Most groups will have invested a fair amount of money and effort into readying each prospective adoptee. Greyhounds will usually have been neutered or spayed, dewormed, and vaccinated, and often checked for tick-borne parasites and had a tooth cleaning while under anesthesia. They may also come equipped with a leash and collar and perhaps this book. They may have been transported over hundreds of miles and fed and housed for months. Although many groups receive funding through the AGC, adoption fees are also needed to defray their costs.

Before going further, step back and fully consider what you are doing. A dog is not a trial-run item. A Greyhound is a sentient being that will not understand why he is once again being uprooted from his home or banished to the backyard. He will not understand that his family welcomed him into their home on a whim and then tired of him as the novelty wore off. When you invite a dog into your family, invite him as a real family member, not a passing fancy or a conversation piece. Many people argue that they are doing the ex-racer a favor by saving him from death and that he should be thankful for any home. If that's how you feel you'll do him a bigger favor if you let him find a more committed home.

The NGA Pet Certificate

The NGA offers a pet registration certificate that lists the dog's official NGA name, pet name (optional), color, sex, whelping date, two-generation pedigree, and complete *bertillion*. The bertillion refers to the identification card that every racing Greyhound has on record. It lists his tattoo numbers, and shows his markings from every side, even down to each toenail color. To obtain a pet registration certificate, you must first send your dog's tattoo numbers to the NGA and request a pet-transfer application. You can do this on-line at *http://nga.jc.net/agc/agc.htm* or via mail at the NGA's address (P.O. Box 543, Abilene, Kansas 67410). The tattoo numbers will be used to identify the owner; you must then send the form to the owner to sign. Be sure to include a self-addressed stamped envelope and tell the owner how thankful you are for your new friend.

If you're having trouble reading your dog's ear tattoos, shine a flashlight through the ear and if that doesn't work, shave the fur off. The right ear number indicates the month and then last digit of the year in which he was born, followed by a letter indicating which pup he was in his litter. The left ear tattoo is his NGA litter registration number.

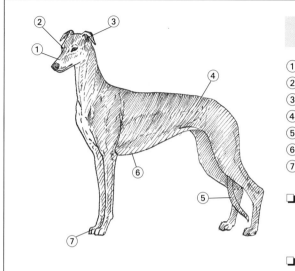

Illustrated Standard

① Long, narrow head
② Scarcely perceptible stop
③ Small, folded ears
④ Well-arched loins
⑤ Tail long, fine, and tapering
⑥ Deep chest
⑦ Hare feet

❏ **Color:** immaterial (includes black, gray, red, fawn, either solid or brindled, either whole colored or spotted)
❏ ***DQ:** none

*DQ = disqualification

Why You Can't Breed Your Greyhound

With the hordes of Greyhounds clamoring to be adopted, it's not only difficult to justify breeding more, but also foolhardy to think that potential puppy owners would beat a path to your door.

Most ex-racers are neutered before being made available for adoption, and the NGA will not register puppies from adopted Greyhounds; the owner would have kept the dog for breeding had it been breeding quality. And most AKC breeders will sell pets only with the agreement that they be neutered.

Caution: Unless you are an established breeder of show or coursing Greyhounds, count on keeping every newborn puppy for the rest of its life. If you balk at keeping ten Greyhounds for the next decade, you had best heed the following advice: Never, *never*, be tempted to breed a litter of Greyhounds.

SOCIAL GRACES

Your Greyhound now faces the transition from kennel dog to family member. Every day will be full of novel experiences and new rules. Your Greyhound may be overly cautious of some everyday items and oblivious to the real dangers of others. She will need your help in being introduced to this brave new world. Teaching your Greyhound new skills is both fun and easy.

Rest and Relaxation

Greyhounds haven't been dubbed the "forty-mile-per-hour couch potato" for nothing. They have turned relaxation into an art form, and their palette is your furniture. Even fat Greyhounds don't have the body padding to enable them to be comfortable on a cold, hard, floor, so don't expect your Greyhound to sleep off the furniture unless you provide him with his own warm soft spot. Some people give their Greyhounds a certain chair, others train them to get on the sofa only if a special blanket is on it, and others provide a snug bed inside a cage. A bean-bag chair or a "pappa-san" chair cushion make excellent Greyhound roosts. The best way to keep your dog off the furniture is to spend time with your dog on the floor, then guide her to her own sumptuously soft bed when she's on your furniture. But a warning: Choose your battles carefully. You will never win if you think you'll keep your Greyhound off all your furniture while you're away from home.

Greyhounds add a touch of elegance to any home.

Private quarters: Your Greyhound will probably appreciate the soothing familiarity of a cage. She is used to sleeping and eating in her own personal cage, and may find it easier to adjust if she has this home base. A cage also makes housebreaking easier, as your Greyhound almost certainly won't soil her cage. But don't expect your Greyhound to stay in a cage all day, every day, while you are at work. This may be close to the life your Greyhound is used to, but remember, when at the kennels other dogs and people were usually present. There's a difference between being alone in a cage with nothing to see and being in one with a floor show available. A cage should be the canine equivalent of a toddler's crib: a place for naptime where you can leave your dog without fear of her hurting herself or your home. It is not a place for punishment, nor is it a storage box for your dog when you're through playing with her.

Hard beds and hygromas: Greyhounds have little covering over their bones and can develop fluid-filled sacs, called *hygromas*, over pressure points if they do not have soft bedding. Small hygromas can be treated with ice packs and

Creature Comforts

Your welcome basket should include:

✔ Buckle collar: for wearing around the house.

✔ Martingale collar: for wearing on walks; Greyhounds can back out of buckle collars.

✔ Leash: nylon, web, or leather, but never chain, which is too hard to hold.

✔ Lightweight retractable leash (optional): Be sure not to drop the leash as it can retract toward the dog and frighten her.

✔ Stainless steel food and water bowls: avoid plastic; it can cause allergic reactions and hold germs.

✔ Cage (optional): large enough for an adult to stand up in. Plastic cages are inexpensive, airline approved, and can be taken apart so the bottom can be used as a bed. Wire cages allow better ventilation and view, and fold for easy storage.

✔ Toys: latex squeakies, fleece-type toys, ball, stuffed animals, stuffed socks, empty plastic milk or soda jugs. Make sure no parts of toys, including squeakers or plastic eyes, can be pulled out and swallowed.

✔ Chewbones: the equivalent of a teething ring for babies.

✔ Baby gates: better than a shut door for placing parts of your home off limits. Do not use the accordion-style gates, which a dog can get its head stuck in and asphyxiate.

✔ Soft brush.

✔ Nail clippers: guillotine type is easier to use.

✔ Poop scoop: two-piece rake type is best for grass.

✔ Dog shampoo (see page 37 for choices).

✔ First aid kit (see page 82 for contents).

✔ Food: start with the same food the dog is currently eating (see page 29 for options).

✔ Dog bed: a round cushion is heavenly, but you can also use a well-padded cage bottom.

✔ Sweater or coat for cold weather.

✔ Secure fence: the first necessity if you want to leave your Greyhound in your yard.

✔ Child's wading pool (optional): great for playing and cooling off in hot weather.

softer bedding; more advanced ones may need veterinary attention. Left untreated, they can become permanently enlarged and hardened; some can even become ulcerated and develop into bedsores.

Greyhounds and Other Pets

Greyhounds are by nature amiable and not inclined to fight with other dogs. They form close attachments to their housemates and will play and run together until exhausted when given a chance. Ex-racers are used to the constant presence of other dogs and may be very lonely at first. Consider adding another pet if you are away for most of the day. In fact, while in many ways two dogs are better than one, three dogs can be better than two! With two dogs a problem can arise when one is left alone while you train or give personal attention to the other. With three there is always a pair left. Are four dogs better than three? No. Four dogs make one dog too many to catch and hold onto while walking off lead.

When introducing new dogs to each other, it is best if both are taken to a neutral site so that territoriality does not evoke protectiveness. An ideal way for dogs to accept each other is to have two people each walking a dog beside each other as they would on a regular walk.

Cats: Greyhounds can get along with cats, but they need to be introduced cautiously. Some ex-racers may have live coursing experience, and although they can discriminate cats from rabbits, you need to give them a chance to see up close that there is a difference. From behind, a running cat looks a lot like a lure. Avoid letting the cat run from the dog; this would evoke a chase response. Dog-cat introductions are best made indoors, initially with a leash and muzzle. Let the dog see you hold, pet, and feed the cat, and then pet and feed the dog a wonderful treat. If the dog is fed every time the cat appears, she will come to really appreciate the cat. Many Greyhounds have become fast friends with "their" pet cats, but until you are absolutely sure of your Greyhound's behavior, do not leave the two loose home alone or outdoors.

Water the Lawn— Not the Floors!

Your Greyhound probably already understands the basics of house-training. She is used to staying in her cage and waiting for each of several daily turnouts outside to relieve herself. This is why using a cage will aid you in house-training your Greyhound. Even if you don't have a cage, you can make the best of your Greyhound's habits by keeping her in a confined area and letting her out many times a day. You must go outside with your dog every time. She is very confused and dependent on you, and may just huddle by the door until you let her back inside. Don't take her for a walk; don't play with her; simply go with her to her relief area, say "*Hurry up,*" and be ready to

praise her and even give her a treat when she does her deed.

Punishing a dog for a mess she has made earlier is totally fruitless; it only succeeds in convincing the dog that every once in a while, for no apparent reason, you are apt to go insane and attack her. It is a perfect recipe for ruining a trusting relationship. That "guilty" look you may think your hound is exhibiting is really fear that you have once again lost your mind.

Accidents

If your previously house-trained Greyhound begins to soil the house, it warrants a physical examination to consider the following possibilities:

✔ Older Greyhounds may lose bladder control; a doggy door or absorbent bedding can help keep your home cleaner.

✔ Older spayed females often become incontinent; drug therapies may help.

✔ Urinary tract infections can cause dogs to urinate small amounts suddenly and frequently; over-the-counter human remedies often help as a first try; otherwise, prescription drugs are needed.

✔ Greyhounds that have accidentally soiled the house often continue to soil the same area; the area must be deodorized with an enzymatic cleaner—available at a pet supply store—and the dog kept out of it for a while.

✔ Intact, and to a lesser extent, castrated male Greyhounds that mark inside the house are difficult to cure; deodorizers and dog-deterring odorants may help. Some owners resort to using bellybands with absorbent diapers on incorrigible males.

✔ Submissive Greyhounds may urinate upon greeting you; punishment only makes this "submissive urination" worse. Don't use dominating

Because they have little body fat, thin fur, and a large body surface to volume ratio, Greyhounds get cold easily and appreciate a snuggly coat in chilly weather.

Some Greyhounds that are used to using a sand or gravel paddock for their "business" may be initially confused about what you expect them to do on your pretty lawn.

signals with these dogs and greet them calmly. Increasing the dog's confidence is the best cure.

✔ Greyhounds that soil only when left alone may be suffering from separation anxiety: treating the anxiety is the best cure (see page 25).

✔ Greyhounds that soil only when left in a cage may be suffering from cage anxiety; they may do better if left loose in a dog-proof room.

Stairs Step-by-Step

The world of the racing Greyhound is pretty much flat, with the possible exception of a leap into an upper-berth cage. So when it comes to those funny places where the floor zigzags up and over, it's only natural that any Greyhound with good sense keeps her feet well away from such aberrant footing. With a little help, however, your Greyhound can master the dreaded stairs.

1. Start with beginner-type stairs: short flights with nonskid surfaces and closed backs. Start by going up, not down, which is trickier.

2. Put your Greyhound on a short leash and walk beside her. You may need to tap the step or even *place* her feet on it. Urge her up one step at a time. When going up, if you can start near the top of the steps it's sometimes easier than starting at the bottom, as the goal of level ground is close. Place a treat at the top of the steps to give your dog extra incentive. An especially nervous dog may feel more comfortable if you or a helper steady her around her loin or rump area.

3. When going down steps, try to start near the bottom. The combination of the Greyhound's long legs and forward center of gravity makes going down steps more difficult. Keep your Greyhound on a short lead and walk next to her head.

4. Don't ever just pull your dog up or down the steps; she's likely to leap and stumble. Don't let her fall, turn around, or bound up or down. She must take them one by one. Work up to longer flights, always on lead at first. Your stairs should be covered with a nonskid surface.

"Grey" Areas of Misbehavior

Even great Greys can be bad. Before despairing consult a Greyhound adoption group or a certified canine behaviorist. The latter may employ a combination of conditioning and drug therapy to achieve a cure. A thorough veterinary exam is first needed to rule out physiological causes.

Sometimes misbehavior is made worse through the overuse of punishment. If punishment doesn't work the first time, why would it work the second, third, or fourth time?

Home Destruction

One of the most common Greyhound behavior problems is home redecoration. Greyhounds are social dogs that have spent their lives in the company of trainers and other Greyhounds. A Greyhound that now finds herself a beloved pet tends to become extremely dependent on her new human family. Left alone, she feels separated from her pack and may feel deserted and frightened. She may react by becoming agitated, drooling and panting, and by trying to escape from confinement. Perhaps she reasons that if she can just get out of the house she will be reunited with her people. The telltale signature of a dog suffering from separation anxiety is that most of the destructive behavior is focused around doors and windows.

✔ Treatment consists of leaving the dog alone for very short periods of time. Work up to

A martingale collar, such as this Greyhound is wearing, is a necessity for Greyhound safety. A mesh kennel muzzle can be a helpful safety aid when introducing your Greyhound to cats and small animals.

"Who us? Eat your chair?" You bet!

longer periods, taking care that the dog never becomes anxious.

✔ A veterinary prescription drug (clomipramine—a tricyclic antidepressant) is available that can help calm your dog and facilitate training.

✔ A tired dog has less energy to devote to redecorating; if possible, run your dog hard and then give her a chance to settle down to nap before leaving her alone.

✔ Give her a puzzle toy—one that requires her to work at getting food out of it—to distract her.

✔ Try to diminish cues that signal you're not home. Don't get in the habit of turning off the television or radio just before you leave; leave them on if they're usually on.

✔ Refrain from a big farewell or joyous reunion. Upon your return, no matter what the condition of the home, greet the dog calmly or even ignore her for a few minutes, to emphasize the point that being left was really no big deal.

TIP

Greyhound Grins and Growls

✔ A wagging tail and lowered head signals submission.

✔ A lowered body, wagging tucked tail, urination, and perhaps even rolling over signals extreme submission.

✔ Yawning, drooling, and panting signal nervousness (or carsickness).

✔ A high, rigidly held tail, raised hackles, stiff, upright posture, and direct stare signal challenging behavior.

✔ A wagging tail, front legs and elbows on the ground, and rear in the air signal playful behavior.

Fearfulness

Racing Greyhounds are expected to be brave. Those that were afraid of other dogs, strangers, and crowds usually find their way to adoption quickly. Even Greyhounds that were brave at the track are faced with a new world they've never experienced. Most of them will learn to cope, but some remain apprehensive.

Although usually happy to meet new friends, the Greyhound is naturally a bit cautious. Don't force a dog that is afraid of people to be petted by somebody she doesn't know. Strangers should ignore shy dogs. When the dog gets braver, have the stranger offer her a tidbit, at first while not even looking at the dog. Staring a dog directly in the eye is interpreted as a threat. It can cause a fearful dog to bite.

Aggression: Biting is unusual in Greyhounds, and is often fear related. A scared dog with no route of escape will often bark, growl, or bite out of perceived self-defense. Introduce dogs and children carefully, encouraging the child to be gentle and to offer the dog a treat. Teach children not to stare at strange dogs or to run from them.

Jumping Up

Teach your Greyhound to sit and stay so that you can kneel down to her level for greetings. When your Greyhound does jump up, simply say "No" and step backward, so that her paws meet only air. Teaching your dog a special command that lets her know it's OK to jump up can actually help her discriminate the difference.

Cat Chasing

You almost certainly will be unable to teach your Greyhound to refrain from chasing the

CHECKLIST

Home Training Guidelines

1 Punishment Doesn't Work: Striking, shaking, choking, and hanging are extremely dangerous, counterproductive, and cruel; they have no place in the training of a beloved family member.

Plus, punishment doesn't work.

2 Correct and Be Done with It: Owners sometimes try to make this "a correction the dog will remember" by ignoring or chastising the dog for the rest of the day. The dog may indeed remember that her owner was upset, but she will not remember why. The dog will only associate her current behavior with your immediate reactions.

3 You Get What You Ask For: Dogs repeat actions that bring them rewards whether you intend for them to or not. Letting your Greyhound out of her cage to make her stop whining might work momentarily, but in the long run you will end up with a dog that whines incessantly every time you put her in a cage. Make sure you reward only those behaviors you want to see more often.

4 Mean What You Say: Lapses in consistency are ultimately unfair to the dog. If you feed your dog from the table "just this one time" because she begs, you have taught her that while begging may not always result in a handout, you never know—it just might pay off tonight. And this intermittent payoff produces behavior that is most resistant to change. You could hardly do a better job of training your Greyhound to beg if you tried.

5 Say What You Mean: Your Greyhound takes commands literally. If you have taught her that "*Down*" means to lie down, then what must she think when you yell "*Down*" to tell her to get off the sofa where she was already lying down? Think before you speak.

6 Think Like a Dog: Dogs live in the present; if you punish them they can only assume it is for their behavior at the time of punishment. So if you discover a mess, drag your dog to it from her nap in the other room, and scold, she will assume that either she is being scolded for napping or you are mentally unstable.

neighbor's cat. A cat, especially a strange one, running outside is too great a temptation. That's one reason your Greyhound shouldn't be unleashed even in your front yard. You may or may not be able to teach your Greyhound to respect your own cat, but running cats and Greyhounds don't mix outdoors.

Remember: The only perfectly behaved dog is a stuffed one—but they're not nearly as fun and loving as a Greyhound, even if the living version does occasionally get into trouble.

If you follow these training techniques carefully, your Greyhound's behavior should be relatively problem-free.

FAST FOOD

Your Greyhound's performance, health, and longevity depend in part upon what you choose to feed. Because most dogs are usually fed one type of food, it makes choosing the best diet even more important and intimidating. The subject of the best diet is filled with controversy.

Commercial Versus Home-Prepared Diets

The first point of contention is whether dogs are better off being fed commercially prepared diets versus home-prepared diets.

Proponents of commercial diets point out that these foods have been tested on generations of dogs and are constantly adjusted to provide optimal nutrition, and that premium-grade foods contain human-quality ingredients. Critics of commercial diets point out that these foods are highly processed, do not resemble a dog's natural diet, are not fresh, and may use ingredients unfit for human consumption.

Home-prepared diets can include cooked or raw foods. Raw food diets advocate more natural feeding by giving dogs whole raw animal carcasses. Proponents point out that such diets are more like the natural diet of ancestral dogs, and claim good health, clean teeth, and

Your Greyhound may have a different idea of culinary delights and good nutrition from yours.

economical food bills. Detractors point out that, while the raw diet may be closer to what wolves eat, dogs are no longer wolves and haven't lived off the land for thousands of generations. Controlled studies on the safety and efficacy of such diets have yet to be published. Critics worry that raw foods from processing plants may pose the threat of salmonella and *E. coli*, although dogs are more resistant to illness from them compared to people.

Cooked homemade diets provide a variety of nutrients in fresh foods according to accepted nutrition standards for dogs. Ask your veterinarian to suggest a source for home-prepared menus.

No matter which diet you choose, you need to understand some basics of canine nutrition.

Evaluating Commercial Foods

If you choose to feed commercial food, feed a high-quality food from a name-brand company. Always strive to buy and use only the freshest food available. Dry food loses nutrients as it sits, and the fat content can become rancid.

Dogs are omnivorous, meaning their nutritional needs can best be met by a diet derived from both animals and plants. These nutrients are commercially available in several forms.

Dry food (containing about 10 percent moisture): This is the most popular, economical, and healthy, but least enticing form.

Semimoist foods (with about 30 percent moisture): These contain high levels of sugar used as preservatives. They are tasty, convenient, and very handy for traveling, but are not an optimal nutritional choice as a regular diet.

Canned food: This has a high moisture content (about 75 percent), and is tasty but not economical.

Canine Nutrition

A good rule of thumb is that three or four of the first six ingredients of a dog food should be animal derived. These tend to be tastier and more highly digestible than plant-based ingredients; more highly digestible foods generally mean less stool volume and fewer gas problems.

When comparing food labels, keep in mind that differences in moisture content make it difficult to make direct comparisons between the guaranteed analyses in different forms of food unless you first do some calculations to equate the percentage of moisture. The components that vary most from one brand to another are protein and fat percentages.

Protein

Protein provides the necessary building blocks for growth and maintenance of bones,

TIP

4D Meat

Racing Greyhounds eat a high-protein diet typically consisting of about a pound (.5 kg) of raw "4D" meat—meaning meat from diseased, disabled, dying, and dead cattle—mixed with an equal amount of high-protein kibble, plus vegetables, milk, and other additives. In some rare cases Greyhounds have become severely ill and even died from eating raw meat; a fatal condition called "Alabama rot" has been linked to food poisoning from 4D meat. In most cases, however, dogs eat 4D meat and remain quite healthy.

muscle, and coat, and in the production of infection-fighting antibodies. The quality of protein is as important as its quantity. Meat-derived protein is higher quality and more highly digestible than plant-derived protein; eggs have the highest level of digestible protein of any source. This means that two foods with identical protein percentages can differ in the nutritional level of protein according to the protein's source.

Most Greyhounds will do fine on regular adult foods having protein levels of about 22 to 27 percent (dry food percentage). Stressed, highly active, or underweight dogs should be fed higher protein levels. A typical racing diet consists of about 27 to 30 percent protein. It was once thought that older dogs should be fed low-protein diets in order to avoid kidney problems, but it's now known that high-protein diets do not cause kidney failure. In fact, high-quality protein is essential to dogs with compromised kidney function. Such dogs should have reduced phosphorus levels, however, and special diets are available that satisfy these requirements.

Fat

Fat is the calorie-rich component of foods, and most dogs prefer the taste of foods with higher fat content. Fat is necessary to good health, aiding in the transport of important vitamins and providing energy. Dogs deficient in fat—usually from diets containing less than 5 percent dry matter fat—may have sparse, dry coats and scaly skin. Excessive fat intake can cause obesity and appetite reduction, creating a deficiency in other nutrients. Most Greyhounds do well on a diet containing about 10 to 15 percent dry food percentage fat. Obese dogs or dogs with heart problems, pancreatitis, or diarrhea should be fed a low-fat food.

Carbohydrates

Carbohydrates are a fairly inexpensive source of nutrition and make up a large part of most commercial dog foods. Carbohydrates in most dog foods are primarily plant derived. Many carbohydrates are poorly utilized by the dog's digestive system. Those derived from rice are best utilized, those from potato and corn far less so, and wheat, oat, and beans even less again. Cooking increases the nutrient availability. Excessive amounts of carbohydrates in the diet can cause decreased performance, diarrhea, and flatulence.

Fiber

Fiber in dog food varies considerably. Typical Greyhound diets contain about 5 percent fiber. Better-quality fiber sources include beet pulp and rice bran, but even these should provide a small percentage of a food's ingredients. Too much fiber interferes with digestion and can cause diarrhea or larger stool volume. Weight-reducing diets often include larger amounts of fiber so the dog will feel more full and to prevent digestibility of some of the other nutrients (see page 34).

A dog's optimal level of each nutrient will change according to his age, energy requirements, and state of health. Prescription commercial diets and recipes for home-prepared diets are available for dogs with various illnesses or needs.

Feeding and Weight

Rather than leaving food always available, it's usually better to feed your dog on a schedule so you can notice if his appetite is off. Adult dogs can be fed once a day, but two smaller meals a day is preferable. All dogs

TIP

Never Feed
✔ Any bones that can be swallowed. They can cause choking or intestinal blockage, or their sharp ends can pierce the stomach or intestinal walls. Cooked or dry bones are more likely to break and splinter.
✔ Mineral supplements, unless advised to do so by your veterinarian.
✔ Chocolate. It contains theobromine, which is poisonous to dogs.
✔ Onions. They can break down red blood cells.

Any Greyhound knows the best food is found on your table when your back is turned.

Sharing an occasional treat is fun, and usually okay.

Less active dogs need lower calorie foods.

Active dogs need more energy-packed foods.

Hungry eyes are hard to resist . . .

Plenty of clean, fresh water is essential to your dog's health—but a dog bowl is better.

Every dog has a unique metabolism. Different dogs will require different diets to maintain their optimal physiques.

have different metabolism, so each dog's diet must be adjusted accordingly.

Weight Reduction Diets

The Greyhound is an athlete, and should have a lean, muscular body. A Greyhound should have a small waist; ribs should be easily felt through a layer of muscle. Many new Greyhound owners are not accustomed to their normal lean bodies and work diligently to fatten them up. Obesity predisposes dogs to joint injuries and heart problems and makes many preexisting problems worse.

Overweight Greyhounds should be fed a lower-calorie diet. Commercially available diet foods supply about 15 percent fewer calories per pound. The role of high fiber in reducing diets is controversial; recent studies suggest it does not provide the lowered hunger perception it was once thought to. Newer research has shown that diet foods relatively high in protein are more effective. Home-prepared diets are available that are both tasty and less fattening.

One of the many pleasures of living with a Greyhound is sharing a special treat, so substitute a low-calorie alternative such as rice cakes, carrots, or other vegetables. Keep your dog out of the kitchen or dining area at mealtimes. Schedule a walk immediately following your dinner to get your dog's mind off your leftovers—it will be good for both of you.

If your dog remains overweight, seek your veterinarian's opinion. In fact, your dog should be checked before embarking on any serious weight reduction effort. Heart disease and some endocrine disorders, such as hypothyroidism or Cushing's disease, or the early stages of diabetes, can cause the appearance of obesity and should be ruled out or treated. A dog that has only the stomach enlarged, without fat around the shoulders or rump, is especially suspect and should be examined by a veterinarian. However, most fat Greyhounds are simply fat!

Weight Gaining Diets

It's more unusual to see a skinny Greyhound. A dog that loses weight rapidly or steadily for no apparent reason should be taken to the veterinarian. Several diseases, including cancer, can cause wasting.

A few dogs just don't gain weight well, and some are just picky eaters. Underweight dogs may gain weight with puppy food; add water, milk, bouillon, ground beef, or canned food, and heat slightly to increase aroma and palatability. Milk will cause many dogs to have diarrhea, so try only a little bit at first. Of course, once you start this you know you're making your picky eater pickier!

A sick or recuperating dog may have to be coaxed into eating. Cat food or meat baby food are both relished by dogs and may entice a dog without an appetite to eat. Try cooking chicken breasts or other meat, but ask your veterinarian first.

Gastric Dilatation Volvulus (GDV)

Also called *bloat*, GDV is a life-threatening emergency in which gas and fluid become trapped in the stomach. It is most common in large breeds with deep, narrow chests. Stress seems to precipitate a bloating episode. Dogs with stable temperaments and dogs that eat some canned food and table scraps are less likely to bloat.

To be on the safe side, avoid other suspected risk factors, which means you should

CHECKLIST

Feeding Checklist

The performance, health, and longevity of your Greyhound, in large part, depend on what you feed it. As most dogs are usually fed only one type of food, selection of the most nutritional and well-balanced diet is crucial.

1 Controversy exists as to whether commercial dog foods are better than home-prepared meals. Proponents of commercial diets point out that these foods have been extensively tested and adjusted to provide the highest nutritional values. Homemade diets, which can include cooked and raw foods, are more like a dog's natural diet, according to proponents. Whether you choose to purchase commercial dog food or prepare your own, it is important that you understand some basic concepts of dog nutrition.

2 When feeding a commercial diet, make sure you choose a high-quality, name-brand product. Feed only the freshest food available, as nutrients lose their potency and ingredients may become rancid with age. Commercial dog food comes in a variety of forms, including dry, semimoist, and canned.

3 When comparing labels on commercial foods, remember that differences in moisture content make it difficult to make direct comparisons among the numerous brands currently available. The most important components to check include protein, fat, carbohydrates, and fiber.

4 It is preferable to feed your dog on a schedule rather than having food always available. Adult dogs can be fed once a day, but two smaller meals a day are preferable. As all dogs have different rates of metabolism, each dog's diet must be adjusted accordingly.

5 Overweight Greyhounds should be fed a lower-calorie diet. Commercially available diet foods supply about 15 percent fewer calories per pound. Underweight dogs may gain weight with puppy food supplemented with items like bouillon, ground beef, or canned food.

6 Never feed your dog bones that can be swallowed. They can cause choking and intestinal blockage, or their sharp ends can pierce the walls of the stomach or intestines.

✔ feed several small meals instead of one large meal.

✔ include some canned food or table scraps.

✔ not allow the dog to gulp food.

✔ not allow your dog to be stressed around his mealtime.

✔ premoisten food, especially foods that expand when moistened.

Water

Water is essential for your Greyhound's health and comfort. Empty, scrub, and refill the water bowl daily; merely topping it off gives algae and bacteria a chance to multiply. Most dogs, especially sick ones, appreciate ice cubes added to the water. Be forewarned that many Greyhounds view the toilet bowl as a deluxe water fountain!

GREAT GREY GROOMING

One of the appeals of Greyhounds is the pleasure derived simply from stroking their silken coat— an experience made even more pleasurable when that coat is clean and healthy. Just as with people, good grooming involves more than an occasional brushing of the hair. Keeping the nails, teeth, eyes, and ears well groomed is important not just for beauty's sake, but for health.

Coat Care

The Greyhound coat is relatively low maintenance. A quick once-over with a soft brush or damp cloth will usually be enough to loosen dirt and impart a good sheen to the hair. Dogs kept indoors under artificial lighting shed year-round, with a major shedding season in the spring. A daily vigorous brushing during shedding season, using a bristle or rubber curry brush, is the best way to hurry along shedding. More hairs will shed after bathing, and dead hairs are especially easy to dislodge when the coat is almost, but not quite yet, dry.

Bathing and Drying

You can keep your Greyhound fairly clean without bathing, but she really will be nicer to hold close if she is bathed occasionally. Between baths you can clean her with a rinse-free shampoo. These are shampoos that are applied to the coat and then simply rubbed dry. For the best results, however, nothing takes the place of a real bath.

The picture of good grooming.

Shampoo selection: The best shampoo is dog shampoo. Canine and human hair have different pH values and so need different shampoos. Dog skin has a pH of 7.5, while human skin has a pH of 5.5; bathing in a shampoo formulated for the pH of human skin can lead to scaling and irritation. However, if your dog has a healthy coat and you just want a simple bath, using a human shampoo is fine.

Bathing: The easiest place to wash your Greyhound is in a bathtub with a hand-held sprayer. Place a nonslip rubber pad on the bottom so she will feel more comfortable. Warm the room beforehand and use warm water to avoid chilling your dog. Warm water also tends to open the hair follicles and helps loosen dead hair. Keep one hand under the spray so you can monitor the water temperature.

Start by wetting down the dog to the skin, leaving the head for last. Mix the shampoo with water first. Work up a moderate lather. Don't let water get into the ears, or shampoo into the eyes. Rinsing is a crucial step; shampoo remaining in the coat can cause dryness and itchiness.

Begin rinsing from the front and top of the dog and work toward the back and rear.

Drying: Have a towel ready for initial drying. Don't let your dog outside on a chilly day when still damp from a bath. You have removed the oils from the coat and saturated your dog down to the skin, making the dog actually wetter—and colder—than she would be from swimming.

Trimming

Even in the show ring, very little trimming is required or even desired. Errant hairs can be snipped off and the underside of the tail can be neatened, but there's really little to do on most dogs. Some dogs carry a thicker coat, and a rubber shedding mitt or large rubber bristle brush may help pull out undercoat.

Skin Problems

Grooming gives you the chance to examine the condition of the skin. Skin problems can be uncomfortable and unsightly, and often lead to hair loss. Problems can result from parasites, allergies, bacteria, fungus, endocrine disorders, and a long list of other possible causes.

Dandruff: Many Greyhounds have dandruff, and it's especially noticeable on dark dogs. Dandruff can have several causes. It occurs more often in winter when indoor heating dries the skin. Keep your dog well hydrated by offering tasty liquids to drink. Wash her with a shampoo containing salicylic acid or sulfur. Follow the bath with a crème rinse to seal in moisture. Use one with colloidal oatmeal if the dog's skin is dry and itchy. Sometimes adding a fish oil capsule to the diet can help. To remove dandruff use a flea comb—available at a pet supply store—or wipe the coat with a nylon stocking.

Bad odor: Generalized bad odor can indicate a skin problem, such as seborrhea. Also check the mouth, ears, feet, anus, and genitals for infection. A far too common cause is smelly saliva from bad teeth; the dog licks herself and the entire dog then smells. Impacted anal sacs can also contribute to bad odor. Don't ignore bad odor, and don't make your dog take the blame for something you need to fix. Consult your veterinarian.

Skin allergies: Flea allergy dermatitis (FAD) is the most common of all skin problems. Even a single fleabite to a susceptible dog causes an allergic reaction to the flea's saliva that results in intense itching, not only in the vicinity of the flea bite, but often all over the dog and especially on its rump, legs, and paws. The dog chews these areas and causes irritation leading to crusted bumps.

Besides FAD, dogs can have allergic reactions to pollens or other inhaled allergens. Canine inhalant allergies usually result in itchy skin, typically first appearing in young dogs and worsening with age. The main sites of itching are the face, ears, feet, forelegs, armpits, and abdomen. Dogs can also have food allergies that can cause itching.

Allergens can be isolated with an intradermal skin test, in which small amounts of various allergen extracts are injected under the skin. The skin is then monitored for localized allergic reactions. Blood tests are also available and are less expensive, but they are not as comprehensive as skin testing. Either test should be performed by a veterinarian with training in the field of allergic skin diseases, as the results can be difficult to interpret.

Bald thigh syndrome: Many racing Greyhounds lose the hair on their outer thighs. As this is one of several commonly seen signs of hypothyroidism, they are often placed on thyroid supplementation. Although this treatment occasionally helps, usually it does not. It has also been theorized that intensive exercise causes hormonal changes that cause hair loss, but even when these dogs are retired to the couch, the bald thighs usually remain. The fact that the hair follicles are completely absent is consistent with the idea that these dogs may have a type of hereditary hair loss, which may in turn be triggered by intensive training.

Calluses: Greyhounds can develop hair loss and calluses on pressure points such as the elbows and chest. Lying on hard surfaces is most likely to cause calluses, but even carpet fibers can wear away hair. Applying skin softeners and keeping your dog on padded surfaces can help.

External Parasites

Parasites remain one of the most common causes of skin and coat problems in dogs. Their damage is more than skin deep, however; many external parasites also carry serious, even deadly, systemic diseases.

Fleas

In any but the mildest of infestations, the new flea control products now available are well worth their initial higher purchase price. It's a lot cheaper to put an expensive product on your dog once every three months than to reapply a cheap one every day.

Traditional flea control products are either less effective or less safe than these newer products. The permethrins and pyrethrins are safe, but have virtually no residual action. The large family of cholinesterase inhibitors (Dursban,

Diazinon, malathion, Sevin, Carbaryl, Pro-Spot, Spotton) are not advisable for use with Greyhounds. Neither should Greyhounds ever wear flea collars. Ultrasonic flea-repelling collars have been shown to be ineffective on fleas and may be irritating to dogs. Brewer's yeast or garlic in the food is equally ineffective.

Always read the ingredients. You may think you're getting a deal with a less expensive product that is applied the same and boasts of the same results as one of the more expensive products, but you're not getting a deal if it doesn't contain the right ingredients. Some of the major ingredients in the newer products are

✔ imidacloprid (for example, Advantage), a liquid applied once a month on the animal's back. It gradually distributes itself over the entire skin surface and kills at least 98 percent of the fleas on the animal within 24 hours and will continue to kill fleas for a month. It can withstand water, but not repeated swimming or bathing.

✔ fipronil (for example, Frontline), which comes as either a spray that you must apply all over the dog's body or as a self-distributing liquid applied only on the dog's back. Once applied, fipronil collects in the hair follicles and then wicks out over time. Thus, it is resistant to being

Fleas and Tapeworms

Fleas transmit the most common tapeworm (Dipylidium) to dogs. Tapeworms look like moving white flat worms when fresh, or like rice grains, usually around the dog's anus, when dried out. Although they are one of the least debilitating of all the worms, their segments can produce anal itching. Tapeworms are not affected by the same kinds of dewormers and preventives as the other common worms.

Getting dried is the best part of bath time—aside from running around like crazy and getting all dirty again.

Pay special attention to your Greyhound's sensitive ears and eyes.

A healthy ex-racer with bald thigh syndrome.

Keeping your Greyhound's teeth clean is one of the most important grooming jobs you can do.

Clean, parasite-free dogs help keep your home clean and pleasant.

Once your Greyhound is perfectly clean and groomed, there's only one thing left to do: Get dirty!

washed off and can kill fleas for up to three months on dogs. It is also effective on ticks for a shorter period.

✔ lufenuron (for example, Program), which is given as a pill once a month. Fleas that bite the dog and ingest the lufenuron in the dog's system are rendered sterile. It is extremely safe; however, all animals in the environment must be treated in order for the regime to be effective.

✔ selamectin (for example, Revolution), which is applied once a month on the dog's back. Some of it enters the bloodstream, some enters the digestive tract, and some redistributes to the skin's sebaceous glands. This wide distribution helps it to be effective against fleas, some ticks, ear mites, sarcoptic mange mites, and heartworms, and it is somewhat effective against hookworms, roundworms, and whipworms.

Ticks

Two newer products for tick control are amitraz collars (tick collars) and fipronil spray or liquid. Neither will keep ticks totally off your dog, but they may discourage them from staying or implanting. Even with these precautions you should check for ticks whenever you are in a potentially tick-infested area.

Ticks can be found anywhere on the dog, but most often burrow around the ears, neck, chest, and between the toes. To remove a tick, use a tissue or tweezers, since some diseases can be transmitted to humans. Grasp the tick as close to the skin as possible, and pull slowly and steadily, trying not to leave the head in the dog. Don't squeeze the tick, as this can inject its contents into the dog. Clean the site with alcohol. Often a bump will remain after the tick is removed, even if you have removed the head. It will go away with time.

Ear Care

The Greyhound's thin ear tips can make them susceptible to several problems. Fly bites can cause irritation, which can lead to scratching, trauma, and even broken blood vessels, and in turn, accumulation of blood in the ear tip. These hematomas should be treated by your veterinarian.

The small capillaries of the ear tips give them relatively poor circulation, rendering them susceptible to chilblains in cold weather. In chilbains, the cells of the ear tips die from lack of oxygen resulting from constriction of blood vessels in cold weather. The dead cells cause itching, bleeding, and ulceration. Using a cut-off sweater sleeve or big sock with the foot cut out to hold the ears snug against the head can keep them warm and healthy in the cold. The itchy, dry, cracked, and even bloody ear tips typical of chilblains can be treated with antibiotics, but veterinary attention is called for if immediate improvement is not seen.

The dog's ear canal is made up of an initial long vertical segment that then abruptly angles to run horizontally toward the skull. This configuration provides a moist environment in which various ear infections can flourish. Fortunately, the Greyhound's folded ears allow for good airflow and ear problems are not common in the breed.

Treating Ear Problems

Ear problems can be difficult to cure once they have become established, so that early veterinary attention is crucial. Signs of ear problems include inflammation, discharge, debris, foul odor, pain, scratching, shaking, tilting of the head, or circling to one side. Bacterial and yeast infections, ear mites or ticks, foreign bodies, inhalant allergies, seborrhea, or hypothyroidism are possible underlying problems. Because the car canal is lined with skin, any skin disorder that affects the dog elsewhere can also strike its ears. Grass awns are a common cause of ear problems in dogs that spend time outdoors. Keep the ear lubricated with mineral oil, and seek veterinary treatment as soon as possible.

If your dog has ear debris, but no signs of discomfort or itching, you can try cleaning the ear yourself, but overzealous cleaning can irritate the skin lining the ear canal. You can buy products to clean the ear or use a homemade mixture of one part alcohol to two parts white vinegar. Hold the ear near its base and quickly squeeze in the ear cleaner—the slower it drips the more it will tickle. Gently massage the liquid downward and squish it all around. Then stand back and let your dog shake it all out (be sure you're outdoors). If the ear has so much debris that repeated rinses don't immediately clean it up, you have a problem that will need veterinary attention. If the ear is red, swollen, or painful, do not attempt to clean it yourself. Your dog may need to be sedated for cleaning, and may have a serious problem. Cleaning solutions will flush debris but will not kill mites or cure infections.

Caution: Don't stick cotton swabs too far down in the ear canal, as they can irritate the skin and pack debris into the horizontal canal. Don't use powders in the ear, which can cake, or hydrogen peroxide, which can leave the ear moist.

Ear Mites

A dog with ear mites will scratch its ears, shake its head, and perhaps hold its head sideways. The ear mite's signature is a dark, dry, waxy buildup resembling coffee grounds in the ear canal, usually in both ears. Sometimes the tiny mites can be seen with a magnifying glass if the material is placed on a dark background.

Separate a dog with ear mites from other pets and wash your hands after handling its ears. Ideally, every pet in a household should be treated. Your veterinarian can provide the best medication. Because ear mites are also found in the dog's fur all over its body, you should treat the dog's fur with a pyrethrin-based shampoo or spray.

Eye Care

Eye care should never be approached with a wait-and-see attitude. Consult your veterinarian at the slightest sign of a problem. Take note of squinting, redness, itching, tearing, dullness, mucus discharge, or any change in pupil size or reactivity. Any time your dog's pupils do not react to light or when one eye reacts differently from another, take her to the veterinarian immediately. It could indicate a serious ocular or neurological problem.

A thick mucus discharge usually indicates a problem that requires veterinary attention. A clear watery discharge can be a symptom of a foreign body, allergies, or a tear drainage problem. A clogged tear drainage duct can cause the tears to drain onto the face, rather than the normal drainage through the nose. Your veterinarian can diagnose a drainage problem with a simple test.

Pannus

Greyhounds are susceptible to pannus, a condition of the clear outer cornea of the eye.

A well-groomed Greyhound looks and feels better.

Even a Greyhound can't outrun fleas and other parasites.

New flea control products cast an invisible net around your dog.

"Oh no! Here she comes with the ear drops again."

Smile!

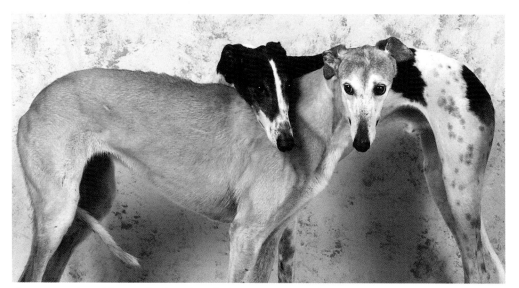

Sometimes the addition of a friend is the best cure—a good excuse to get another Greyhound!

Pannus is usually first noticed as a cloudiness of the cornea, possibly with tears, which progresses over the next few weeks until a thin web of blood vessels spreads inward toward the center of the cornea. It can eventually progress to the point where vision is seriously impaired. Pannus is thought to be an autoimmune condition in which the body attacks its own cells; it is made worse by exposure to ultraviolet light. Treatment involves keeping the dog away from ultraviolet light—keeping her indoors or even fitting her with sunglasses—and treating her eyes with corticosteroids that lower the immune response.

Nail Care

Canine nails evolved to withstand strenuous running and digging. Even though your Greyhound may run around your yard, chances are you're going to need to help keep her nails trimmed. This is especially true for older or more sedate dogs. The most common problem associated with overly long nails occurs when the nail becomes snagged on something, pulling the nail from its bed or dislocating the toe. In addition, overly long nails impact on the ground with every step, causing discomfort and eventually splayed feet and lameness. If dewclaws (the rudimentary "thumbs" on the wrists) are left untrimmed, they can get caught on things even more easily and can be ripped out or actually loop around and grow into the dog's leg. You must prevent this by trimming your dog's nails every week or two. Most exracers are cooperative about having their nails cut; for those that aren't you may have to start gradually or even use a nail grinder.

It's easiest to cut the nails by flexing the foot backward, holding it in the same position in which a blacksmith would shoe a horse. This way your dog can't see what's going on, which often helps calm her.

Use a sharp nail trimmer so that it cuts, rather than crushes, the nail. Be sure to cut off just the hooklike end. Viewed from beneath the nail, you will see a solid core culminating in a hollowed nail. Cut the tip up to the core, but not beyond. On occasion you will slip up and cause the nail to bleed. Apply styptic powder to the nail to stop the bleeding. If this is not available, dip the nail in flour or hold a wet teabag against it. And be more careful next time! Always end a nail trimming session with a treat.

Nail Problems

Some Greyhounds have deformed nails, usually because they grew back in crooked following accidents in which they were pulled from their nail bed. In others, the nails may be affected by an autoimmune condition called pemphigus, in which each nail will swell, often becoming infected, die, and fall off. Immediate veterinary attention is needed to save the nails.

Greyhounds can also get infections of the nail beds, a condition called paronychia. This usually occurs when mud, twigs, or especially sand, has been forced under the cuticle, causing it to become inflamed and painful. Washing the feet and brushing the cuticles with a soft toothbrush after running, or applying a small bandage around susceptible toes, can reduce its incidence.

Dental Care

Correct occlusion is important for good dental health. In a correct Greyhound bite, the top incisors should fit snugly in front of the

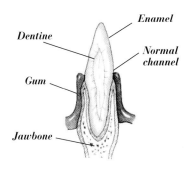

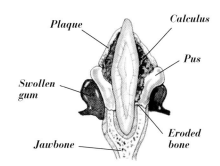

Normal tooth, left, and infected tooth, right.

bottom incisors, with the top canines just behind the bottom canines. Some Greyhounds have a significant overbite, in which the upper incisors are placed well in front of the lower incisors. This may be associated with a condition called base-narrow canines, in which the bottom canines are displaced inward and pierce the palate when the mouth closes. The offending canines may need to be cut down and capped.

The most important dental care you can give your Greyhound is regular teeth brushing. Meat-flavored dog toothpaste helps your dog enjoy the process. Dry food and hard dog biscuits, carrots, rawhide, and dental chewies are only minimally helpful at removing plaque.

If not removed, plaque will attract bacteria and minerals, which will harden into tartar.

Many ex-racers come with a mouth full of tartar. Plaque and tartar are not only unsightly, but contribute to bad breath and health problems. Plaque can cause infections to form along the gum line, then spread rootward causing irreversible periodontal disease with tissue, bone, and tooth loss. The bacteria may also sometimes enter the bloodstream and cause infection in the kidneys and heart valves.

Racing Greyhounds are accustomed to being groomed, and most are very cooperative. A well-groomed Greyhound feels better, looks better, and has a head start on a long and healthy life. You wouldn't want any less for the Greyhound you love.

FAST LEARNERS

Just because your Greyhound is retired doesn't mean he can't learn a new trick or two. For years Greyhounds were never given credit for their intelligence; people equated their narrow heads with narrow minds and thought they were good only for chasing a lure in a circle. They could not have been more wrong.

Quick Studies

True, Greyhounds aren't the typical waggy-tailed obedience stars, and they don't shine if you train them as though they were. Given Greyhound-appropriate methods, though, the typical Greyhound will surprise you with his ability to learn.

Good dog training methods have finally caught up with the techniques successful animal trainers have known for years. Old-fashioned dog training methods based on force are ineffective and no fun for either dog or trainer. Greyhounds are very amenable to training, as long as you use only the gentlest of techniques.

You don't have to go to obedience classes to train your Greyhound, although it's certainly an asset if you can find a class that understands the gentle, sensitive nature of Greyhounds. Many classes are geared toward handling boisterous, out-of-control dogs, and may emphasize force methods and lots of

Narrow heads don't mean narrow minds; Greyhounds can be quick studies.

repetition in an attempt to dominate and calm these dogs. Such methods are not good for Greyhounds, and if you can't find an instructor who understands that, you're better off training on your own or with some other Greyhound owners.

The Click Is the Trick

Clicker training is founded on professional animal training techniques and is fast becoming popular with dog trainers. In clicker training you teach the dog that the sound of the clicker signals that a reward is coming. A clicker signal is used because it is fast, noticeable, and something the dog otherwise does not encounter in everyday life. Once the dog associates the click with an upcoming reward, you then wait for him to do the behavior you want him to do. The instant he does so, you click to tell him his behavior is going to pay off. If he makes a mistake, nothing happens. You just wait for him to do it right, giving him guidance when possible. In essence, the dog thinks he's training *you* because he realizes

CHECKLIST

Greyhound Training Tips

1 **Guide, Don't Force:** Greyhounds already want to please you; your job is to show them the way. Forcing them can distract or intimidate them, actually slowing down learning.

2 **Punishment Doesn't Work:** Greyhounds are sensitive and seldom require anything but the mildest of corrections. A direct stare with a harsh "No!" should suffice in most cases.

3 **Working for Food:** Your Greyhound will work better if his stomach is not full, and he will be more responsive to food rewards.

4 **Happy Endings:** Begin and end each training session with something the dog can do well. Keep sessions short and fun—no longer than 10 to 15 minutes.

5 **Your Greyhound Didn't Read the Book:** Nothing will ever go just as perfectly as it seems to in all the training instructions. Just remember to be consistent, firm, gentle, realistic, and most of all, patient.

that whenever he does a certain behavior, he makes you click and then reward him.

Now let's use the clicker to train our Greyhound, Isis, to sit. First we click and then reward Isis several times so she realizes a click means a treat is coming her way. Next we say *"Isis, sit"* and instead of forcing her rear down, we lure her front up by holding a treat above and behind her muzzle. If she jumps up for it, we don't give it to her. Only when she bends her rear legs do we click, and reward. We do it again, clicking and rewarding for successively closer approximations to the *sit* position. Finally Isis sits, we click, we treat; Isis is happy; we're happy. Isis thinks she's the one doing the training; we think we're the ones doing the training—but does it really matter as long as she sits?

We can use the same concept to teach Isis to lie down, come, heel, speak, roll over, or do anything she naturally does on her own. For example, to teach Isis to heel, instead of dragging her back to *heel* position, ignore her until she happens to be in *heel* position for a second. Instantly click and treat, then gradually require her to stay there longer, and add some zigzags and turns, until she discovers being in *heel* position turns you into a human snack machine.

Tools of the Trade

Just as training methods have changed, so has equipment. Gone are the choke collars of the jerk-and-pull school. Positive training methods favor a buckle or preferably a martingale collar, which tightens enough to prevent escape but not as much as a traditional choke collar. A 6-foot (1.8-m) leather or web leash, and a 20-foot (6.1-m) light line complete the Greyhound's training wardrobe.

Training clickers are available from most pet supply catalogs; you can substitute anything small that makes a quick, unusual sound. Your training outfit will need pockets or a treat pouch, and you'll need lots and lots of little treats to put in them. Bits of cat food, semi-moist food, cheese, or dried liver are ideal.

By far the most essential piece of Greyhound training equipment, though, is a bottomless supply of patience and enthusiasm.

Mind Games

You may just find that your Greyhound is gifted and enjoys learning new skills. Obedience clubs offer advanced classes that involve jumping, retrieving, hand signals, and all sorts of challenging exercises. They can also guide you toward earning an obedience title (see below). They are valuable sources of training advice and encouragement from people who are experienced obedience competitors, and provide an environment filled with distractions similar to those you will encounter at actual trials.

Plan on training your greyhound the commands "*Heel*," "*Sit*," "*Down*," "*Come*," and "*Stay*" for use in everyday life. Add the "*Stand for exam*," and your dog will have the basic skills necessary to earn the AKC Companion Dog (CD) title. See "Checklist" (page 54) for a list of what the CD title requires.

Each exercise has points assigned to it, and points are deducted for the inevitable imperfections. No food can be carried into the ring. You must pass each individual exercise to qualify, and to earn the degree you must qualify three times. Higher degrees of Companion Dog Excellent (CDX) or Utility Dog (UD) and Utility Dog Excellent (UDX) also require retrieving, jumping, hand signals, and scent discrimination. The ultimate title, Obedience Trial Champion (OTCh), is awarded for outperforming other dogs at the highest levels of competition.

If you enter competition with your Greyhound, remember this as your Golden Rule: Companion Dog means just that; being upset at your dog because he made a mistake defeats the purpose of obedience as a way of promoting a harmonious partnership between trainer and dog. Failing a trial, in the scope of life, is

TIP

Citizen Canine

In order to formally recognize dogs that behave in public, the AKC offers the Canine Good Citizen (CGC) certificate, which requires your Greyhound to do the following:

✔ Accept a friendly stranger who greets you.
✔ Sit politely for petting by a stranger.
✔ Allow a stranger to pet and groom him.
✔ Walk politely on a loose lead.
✔ Walk through a crowd on a lead.
✔ Sit and lie down on command and stay in place while on a 20-foot line.
✔ Calm down after play.
✔ React politely to another dog; react calmly to distractions.
✔ Remain calm when tied for three minutes in the owner's absence, under supervision by a stranger.

Your Greyhound represents his breed wherever he goes; makes sure he leaves a good impression. His behavior may influence somebody's decision to adopt a Greyhound.

"Will work for food" is the Greyhound's motto.

Your Greyhound will jump at the chance to learn new skills as long as you make it fun.

The Down-Stay is simple for a laid-back Greyhound—as long as the surface is soft and comfortable.

Learning to stand still and stay on command makes posing for photo sessions a breeze—sort of.

The best time to start training is in puppyhood, but it's never too late.

Sometimes a good run is the best reward for a job well done.

☰ CHECKLIST ☰

✔ Heel on lead, sitting automatically each time you stop, negotiating right, left, and about turns without guidance from you, and changing to a faster and slower pace.

✔ Heel in a figure eight around two people, still on lead.

✔ Stand still off lead 6 feet (1.8 m) away from you and allow a judge to touch him.

✔ Do the exercises in number 1, except off lead.

✔ Come to you when called from 20 feet (6.1 m) away, and then return to *heel* position on command.

✔ Stay in a sitting position with a group of other dogs, while you are 20 feet away, for one minute.

✔ Stay in a *down* position with the same group while you are 20 feet away, for three minutes.

an insignificant event. Never let a ribbon or a few points become more important than a trusting relationship with your companion. Besides, your Greyhound will forgive you for the times you mess up!

Tracking

Even a sighthound can follow its nose, and several Greyhounds have demonstrated they can follow a scent trail. The Tracking Dog (TD) title is earned by following a human trail about 500 yards (457 m) long that was laid up to two hours earlier. More advanced titles of Tracking Dog Excellent (TDX), Variable Surface Tracker (VST), and Tracking Champion can also be earned.

Jumping for Joy

The sport of agility combines athletic and mental abilities as dogs jump, sprint, climb, balance, and weave on an obstacle course of tunnels, seesaws, balance beams, jumps, and weave poles. Many obedience clubs are now sponsoring agility training, but you can start some of the fundamentals at home. Entice your dog to walk through a tunnel made of sheets draped over chairs or through a child's play tunnel; guide him with treats to weave in and out of a series of poles made from several plumber's helpers placed in line; make him comfortable walking on a wide raised board; teach him to jump through a tire and over a hurdle. If you can't find a club to train with, you can make your own equipment. Contact the AKC, USDAA, or UKC for regulations.

The Healing Touch

Greyhounds excel at many roles, but perhaps one of the most important is that of canine therapist. Studies have shown that pet ownership increases life expectancy and petting animals can lower blood pressure. In recent years nursing home residents have come to look

Amazing Greys

Ch. El-Aur Aztec CDX, TD, FCh ("Parker" to his friends) was the first Greyhound to earn a tracking title. Parker's dam, Frolic of Aroi, CD may have actually been the first Greyhound to be trained to track, but her untimely death prevented her from adding the title to her name. The first UDT and first TDX Greyhound was Ch Midnight Shadow Traveler UDTX, FCh.

Amazing Greys

The first Greyhound to earn an obedience title was Ch On-Da-Way Skipper CD in 1938. The first Greyhound to earn the utility title was Sheikh, UD—a dog pound rescue whose new owner was told Greyhounds couldn't be trained. The first OTCH and UDX Greyhound was another pound rescue, OTCH The Merry Prankster UDX, TD.

The precocious and talented littermates Ch California Sunshine Traveler UDT, LCM and Ch Midnight Shadow Traveler UDTX, FCh finished their CD titles at the age of seven months and their UD titles at twenty months.

forward to visits by dogs, including many Greyhounds. These dogs must be meticulously well mannered and well groomed. To be registered as a Certified Therapy Dog a dog must demonstrate that he will act in an obedient, outgoing, gentle manner to strangers. Greyhounds possess the perfect blend of attributes for this most vital job: they are amiable without being overwhelming, startlingly beautiful, and perfect for a little hug.

Note: Greyhounds help people in many ways. In Kansas, an innovative program teams correctional facility inmates with Greyhounds for training in preparation for adoption, a relationship that helps everyone involved. Other Greyhounds have been trained in Search and Rescue.

For many Greyhounds, retirement from racing is only the start of a life of adventure, learning, and fun. Many retirees have found fame and happiness off the track.

Amazing Greys

KL's Mandoid From Marze CDX, MX, MXJ is the highest titled agility Greyhound and was the first to earn the OA, OAJ, AX, AXJ, MX, and MXJ titles in AKC agility. Mandoid has maintained her position as the number-one-ranked Greyhound in AKC agility ever since AKC rankings were begun.

THE LOOK OF SPEED

"Grehound shold be heeded lyke a snake
And neckyd lyke a drake,
Backed lyke a beam,
Syded lyke a bream,
Footed lyke a catte,
Taylled lyke a ratte."
—Dame Juliana Berners, Abbess of Sopewell, 1486

So, in Middle English, read the earliest version of the Greyhound standard, the blueprint of the ideal Greyhound. From head to tail, it describes those attributes that make a Greyhound look like a Greyhound. This possession of breed attributes is known as *type*, and has been an important requirement of any Greyhound then and now. A dog should also be built in such a way that it can go about its daily life with minimal exertion and absence of lameness. This equally important attribute is known as *soundness*. Add to these the attributes of good health and temperament, and you have the four cornerstones of the ideal Greyhound.

The AKC Greyhound Standard

Head—Long and narrow, fairly wide between the ears, scarcely perceptible stop, little or no development of nasal sinuses, good length of muzzle, which should be powerful without coarseness. Teeth very strong and even in front.

The Greyhound's form follows its function.

Ears—Small and fine in texture, thrown back and folded, except when excited, when they are semipricked.

Eyes—Dark, bright, intelligent, indicating spirit.

Neck—Long, muscular, without throatiness, slightly arched, and widening gradually into the shoulder.

Shoulders—Placed as obliquely as possible, muscular without being loaded.

Forelegs—Perfectly straight, set well into the shoulders, neither turned in nor out, pasterns strong.

Chest—Deep, and as wide as consistent with speed, fairly well-sprung ribs.

Back—Muscular and broad.

Loins—Good depth of muscle, well arched, well cut up in the flanks.

Hindquarters—Long, very muscular and powerful, wide and well let-down, well-bent stifles. Hocks well-bent and rather close to ground, wide but straight fore and aft.

Feet—Hard and close, rather more hare- than cat-feet, well-knuckled up with good strong claws.

Tail—Long, fine, and tapering with a slight upward curve.

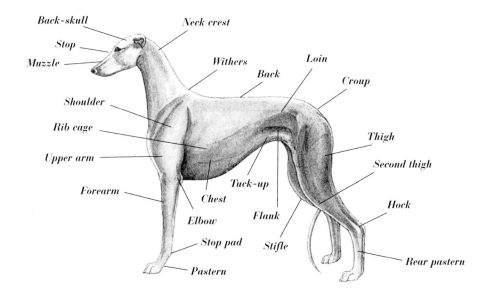

The external parts of the Greyhound.

Coat—Short, smooth, and firm in texture.
Color—Immaterial.
Weight—Dogs, 65 to 70 pounds; bitches, 60 to 65 pounds.

Scale of Points

General symmetry and quality	10
Head and neck	20
Chest and shoulders	20
Back	10
Quarters	20
Legs and feet	20
Total	**100**

What Color Is Your Greyhound?

One of the wonderful things about Greyhounds is the rainbow of colors and patterns available. The American Greyhound Track Operators publishes a chart of the possible colors, but many Greyhounders find it interesting to take an analytical approach to describing Greyhound colors and the genes that control them, as follows:

White

In Greyhounds, there are at least four different alleles (alternate forms of a gene for one trait) for different degrees of white spotting, with more white always recessive to less white. In decreasing order of dominance, the alleles of the S gene are:

✔ **S:** "self-colored," dogs with no white. All such dogs must have at least one copy of S. But because S could mask any of the more recessive alleles, such dogs could be either S/S, S/s^i, S/s^p, or S/s^w.

✔ **sⁱ:** next in dominance, sⁱ causes the so-called "irish-marked" pattern: white feet (and perhaps legs), tail tip, and collar. Such dogs could not have S, but could have one of three allele combinations: either sⁱ/sⁱ, sⁱ/sᵖ, or sⁱ/sʷ.

✔ **sᵖ:** "parti-color": predominantly white with patches of color. Such dogs can be either sᵖ/sᵖ or sᵖ/sʷ.

✔ **sʷ:** mostly white, with a very few or no small patches of color. Because this is the most recessive allele, such dogs would need two copies of it: sʷ/sʷ.

A separate gene controls whether or not there are lots of tiny spots (called ticking) on otherwise white areas. The allele for ticking (T) is dominant to the allele for no ticking (t).

Black

You can think of the white areas on your Greyhound as though a bucket of whitewash had been splashed over the dog, partially obscuring its "true" color beneath. Look beyond any white and see if you notice any pattern of black hair distribution. Black distribution is controlled by several alleles at two different gene locations, A and E, which sometimes interact.

✔ **A:** dominant, results in a pure black dog. Genotype could be A/A or A/aʸ.

✔ **aʸ:** produces a tan or red color. They have the genotype of aʸ/aʸ.

The E series is more complicated:

✔ **Eᵐ:** results in a black muzzle, which would not be visible on a black dog.

✔ **E:** next in dominance, this results in a solid color without a black muzzle.

✔ **eᵇʳ:** results in brindle: irregular vertical black stripes running down the sides of the body over a lighter background.

✔ **e:** dogs with e will have no black hair anywhere, even if they are A/A. In a manner of speaking, it "overrides" the A gene.

Thus, red Greyhounds are ay/ay E/- or aʸ/aʸ Eᵐ/- (where the "–" denotes either Eᵐ, E, eᵇʳ, or e) and fawn Greyhounds are A/A ee or A/aʸ ee.

Saturation

The D gene controls whether colors are diluted:

✔ **D:** dominant; allows intense, fully saturated colors.

✔ **d:** recessive; makes all colors less saturated, and especially makes blacks more gray (or "blue"). Eye color also tends to be lighter.

The C gene also controls dilution of colors:

✔ **C:** dominant; allows intense, fully saturated colors.

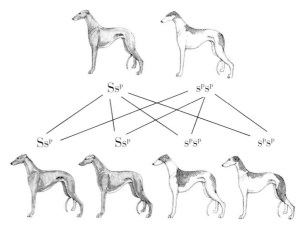

If a solid colored dog carrying a recessive gene for spotting is bred to a spotted dog, on average, half of the offspring will be solid colored and half will be spotted.

Black littermates covered by different amounts of white.

The expression is an integral part of the Greyhound look.

A beautifully built blue brindle.

An unusual tri-colored Greyhound.

Champion form.

A white dog often has a patch of color showing through, usually around the ears or the tail base.

No matter the color, Greyhounds have long been thought of as a sleek and elegant breed.

A Champion Greyhound celebrates at the Westminster Kennel Club show.

Amazing Greys

At the end of a show, one dog alone remains undefeated: the Best in Show winner. It is a feat dreamed of but never attained by most dog show enthusiasts. One Greyhound known as Punky (officially Ch Aroi Talk of the Blues) won not just one, but 68 Best in Shows in her career. Along the way she also won the distinction of the top show dog of any breed in America in 1976.

✔ **c^ch**: recessive; decreases the red or tan coloration while allowing black to remain fully dark black, although its effect is also modified by other genes.

Color is immaterial in either the show ring, the race track, or your heart, but it is an integral part of the special beauty that defines every individual greyhound.

Showing a Greyhound

Conformation shows evaluate your Greyhound on the basis of the official breed standard. A judge will examine each dog from the tip of its nose to the tip of its tail, feeling its body structure, studying its way of moving, and looking at the total picture it creates. If you have gone out of your way to get a show-quality Greyhound, chances are you will want to show her. Most people don't get an ex-racing dog with the idea of showing it, but it, too, can be shown if it has not already been neutered and if you can obtain an AKC registration (not ILP) number.

Greyhounds are a very easy breed to show. There is no fancy grooming and no spiffy showmanship required, but even the best dog needs a little work before showing off. Practice posing your Greyhound with all four feet pointing forward, legs parallel to each other and perpendicular to the ground, and head held high. Your Greyhound should also know how to trot proudly in a dead straight line on a loose show lead (a very thin leash). The most common mistake new handlers make is to demand that their dogs stand like statues for so long that the poor dogs become bored, and then they wonder why the dog hates to show. A happy attitude will overshadow a myriad of faults. Professional handlers can show your dog for you and probably win more often than you would; however, there is nothing like the thrill of winning when you are on the other end of the lead!

Contact your local kennel club or even obedience club and find out if they have handling classes, or when the next match will be held. Matches are informal events where everybody learns: puppies, handlers, even the judges. Win or lose, never take one judge's opinion too seriously, and no matter how obviously feeble-minded you think the judge is, be polite and keep your comments to yourself.

Grooming for the Show Ring

Grooming for the show ring begins long before the show. Long thick winter coats need to go. Use a shedding blade or rubber brush to remove dead hair. Dandruff-prone dogs are best washed a few days, rather than immediately, before the show. A mink oil spray rubbed in on the day of the show can help the coat shine. Cut any straggler hairs, and neaten the hair along the tuck-up and under the tail. Many people cut the vibrissae (whiskers) for a neater and more professional appearance, but leaving these important sensory organs intact is becoming more fashionable.

You, too, must be groomed—you don't want to embarrass your Greyhound. For shows proper attire is a sports jacket for men, skirt or pants suit with flat shoes for women; at matches the dress code is less formal.

Champions

At a real AKC show, each time a judge chooses your dog as the best dog of its sex that is not already a Champion it wins up to five points, depending upon how many dogs it defeats. Unfortunately, in many parts of the country you may have difficulty finding enough competition. To become an AKC Champion (Ch) your Greyhound must win fifteen points, including two majors (defeating enough dogs to win three to five points at a time). You may enter any class for which your dog is eligible: Puppy, Novice, American Bred, Bred by Exhibitor, or Open. The Best of Breed class is for dogs that are already Champions. If you are lucky enough to win Best of Breed, be sure to stick around to compete in the hound group

later in the day. The winner of the hound group then competes with the winner of the other six groups for the Best in Show award.

Rules and Regulations

Before entering you should contact the AKC and ask for the rules and regulations concerning dog shows, which will explain the requirements for each class. Your dog must be entered about three weeks before the show date, and you will need to get a premium list and entry form from the appropriate show superintendent; addresses and show schedules are available from the AKC or most dog magazines (see Information, page 92).

To survive as a conformation competitor you must be able to separate your own ego and self-esteem from your dog; many people cannot do this. You must also not allow your dog's ability to win in the ring cloud your perception of your dog's true worth in her primary role—that of friend and companion. Your Greyhound never has to step foot in a show ring, win a race, earn a title, or thrill anyone except you to have first place in your heart.

LIFE IN THE FAST LANE

Your Greyhound may be retired from racing, but that doesn't mean he has to quit running. Running is part of being a Greyhound, and as a Greyhound owner you're about to be treated to a dog that runs with exhilarating speed. Whether you plan to let your Greyhound sprint around your yard or compete in a running competition, you need to be ready for all the excitement, fun—and dangers—that high-speed running entails.

Running on Course

Coursing differs from racing in that it entails more than simply speed. Historically, the fastest of dogs was of little practical value if he could not control his speed enough to turn after a hare, or could only sustain his speed for a short distance. Competitive coursing entails the subjective judging of a dog's speed, agility, and endurance, as well as some other attributes depending upon whether it is open field coursing or lure coursing.

Open Field Coursing

The sport of coursing, wherein Greyhounds were loosed after hare, was so popular that in the late 1800s the annual Waterloo Cup drew crowds of 80,000. Today, coursing retains a keen, if less populous, following.

Greyhounds love the great outdoors.

In Europe the quarry is the European hare, while in America it is the jackrabbit (actually a hare). Because jackrabbits are found only in the western areas of the United States, most organized open field coursing takes place in the desert regions of California and New Mexico. Greyhounds and their cousins, Salukis, are the major participants. The National Open Field Coursing Association (NOFCA) awards the titles of Coursing Champion (CC) for points won in competition with other sighthounds, and Courser of Merit (CM) for points won in competition only with other Greyhounds. The North American Coursing Association (NACA) also sponsors hunts and awards NACC and NACM titles, comparable to the CC and CM.

Open field coursing requires a tough and committed dog and owner, entails some dangers, a lot of practice and conditioning, and often ends in the death of the quarry. For people who find these aspects unacceptable, the sport of lure coursing provides an alternative.

Lure Coursing

Lure coursing is a simulated course in which a lure—actually a white plastic garbage bag—is dragged at high speed around a system of pulleys. Dogs run in groups of two or three, and are scored on their speed, agility, endurance, enthusiasm, and follow—some wise guys try to outsmart the lure and cut it off at the pass!

Greyhounds fresh off the track are used to running in straight lines and gradual turns. They are invariably surprised the first time the lure makes a sudden turn, and they tend to make very wide turns until they have more experience. Meanwhile you have to take extra precautions to ensure that no obstacles are in place where your wide-running dog could hit them.

The pole lure: Take a pole about 6 feet (1.8 m) long, and attach a string of about the same length to it. On the end of the string attach a lure, either the official plastic garbage bag or a scrap of fur. You can also attach a squawker, which is a simulated rabbit-in-distress call available from hunting stores or from the NGA;

squawkers really get the attention of Greyhounds. Now run around your backyard, whipping the lure around erratically. Let your dog catch the lure occasionally, but quit with your dog still wanting more.

Lure coursing titles: Both the American Kennel Club (AKC) and the American Sighthound Field Association (ASFA) sponsor lure coursing field trials and award titles: the AKC awards the suffix Junior Courser (JC) for a dog that demonstrates he can finish a course running by himself, Senior Courser (SC) for a dog that then demonstrates he can complete a course running alongside another dog on four occasions, and the prefix Field Champion (FC) for dogs that accumulate 15 points in winning against competition. For information contact the American Sighthound Field Association (ASFA), *http://www.asfa.org/* (for the ASFA lure coursing rulebook: *http://www.asfa.org/RuleBook.htm*), or the American Kennel Club (AKC), c/o Dean Wright, Coursing Director, 1235 Pine Grove Rd., Hanover, PA 17331 (for the AKC lure coursing rulebook: *http://www.akc.org/dic/events/perform/lure1.cfm*).

The ASFA also awards a Field Champion (FCh) title, but as a suffix, for dogs that win over several trials against competition, and goes on to award the extremely competitive Lure Courser of Merit (LCM) suffix for continued success against other Field Champions.

Running attire: Your Greyhound will wear a lightweight coursing blanket while competing;

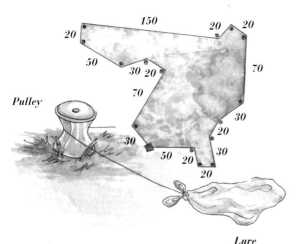

In lure-coursing, the lure is pulled through a field along a string that is looped around several pulleys. The sample course design shown here tests the dogs' speed, agility, and endurance. (Distances are in yards.)

A slip lead is used to release the dog when coursing. By letting go with the right hand, the entire leash and collar will fall away from the dog.

you can borrow one at the trial. Some people will muzzle their dogs, not usually because they bite, but because they catch the lure at the end of the course and won't let go! A muzzle can provide a sort of mouth guard as well, in the event that the lure should ever get caught on a pulley and the dog inadvertently hits the pulley when trying to grab the lure. A racing muzzle works fine. Many Greyhounds run with their front pasterns wrapped in self-clinging leg wraps (such as Vet-Wrap). At full speed, the rear of the pastern actually contacts the ground, and is often abraded or bruised as a result. The large pad of the foot can also be peeled away, a painful but self-healing condition that may be thwarted by wrapping. It's best to ask somebody at the trial to give you a wrapping lesson.

Bring plenty of water, possibly water with electrolytes. In warm weather, bring water in which to soak your dog after running. A terry cloth jacket, made from a towel, can be soaked in water to serve as a cooling blanket on very hot days.

Running Safety

Some owners are reluctant to try racing or coursing because they fear their dog could be injured. In open field coursing the possibility of running into a barbed wire fence or getting lost in the distance are most serious. In lure coursing the greatest danger comes from collisions between dogs or from wide-running dogs that hit trees or other obstacles. Injuries ranging from cuts and broken toes to fatalities have

occurred; fortunately, serious injuries are uncommon. You can do your part to reduce their likelihood.

✔ Do not run your Greyhound competitively if he does not get regular conditioning in the form of running during the week. If your dog has a previous injury, check with your veterinarian to make sure you don't risk reinjuring him. Remember, there is no such thing as halfway for a Greyhound. Once you let him loose after the lure, he will not run at half-speed or run half the distance. Make sure your dog is physically fit and sound or do not run him at all. Always limber up your dog before running, and walk him afterwards. If you expect to compete with your dog in an athletic event, be sure to treat him like the athlete he is.

✔ At a lure coursing trial your Greyhound will be required to complete two runs ("courses") in order to qualify, perhaps more in the event of ties, or if he wins and goes on to compete for Best of Breed, and ultimately Best in Field. Especially with an inexperienced dog, however, you should quit any time your dog appears tired, overheated, sore, or lame.

✔ Any kind of running activity is certainly more dangerous than snoozing on the couch, but everything worth doing in life comes with some risk. Is it worth doing? Ask the people who drive hundreds of miles every weekend to stand in the rain and watch their Greyhound run a course, even though they know their dog may have little chance of winning. They do it because they enjoy watching a beautiful animal do what it does best, and because they enjoy watching their beloved dog do what he loves most.

Back on Track

It may seem peculiar to race a retired racer, but amateur Greyhound racing is purely for fun and many dogs and owners enjoy a trip around a makeshift track. In racing, a group of Greyhounds are all released from a box and are timed until they cross a finish line. Two types of Greyhound racing are popular: straight and oval.

The Large Gazehound Racing Association *(http://www.geocities.com/Petsburgh/2718/)* sponsors straight racing over a 200-yard (183-m) course. Racers earn points toward the Gazehound Racing Champion (GRC) title and then the Superior Gazehound Racing Champion (SGRC) title.

The National Oval Track Racing Association *(http://www.notra.org/)* sponsors oval racing over distances of at least 300 yards (274 m). It awards the titles of Oval Racing Champion (ORC) and Supreme Oval Racing Champion (SORC).

Playing It Safe

You need not attend a racing or coursing event to experience one of the greatest joys of Greyhound ownership—that of watching one of nature's most athletic creations cavorting at Mach speed. Although the Greyhound is one of the more obedient of the sighthound breeds, it is a true sighthound at heart, which means that it was bred to chase first and ask questions later. Thus, you must choose a safe place to run your dog with utmost care.

Everybody thinks his or her dog is smart and trustworthy and reliable off lead. They may be right—until the unpredictable occurs: Another dog attacks, or a cat runs underfoot. Whatever the reason, the trustworthy dog forgets himself for just a moment, and that's all it takes for disaster. Trust is wonderful, but careless trust is deadly. Here are some precautions:
✔ Never unhook the leash until you know everything about the area. Are there so many squirrels and rabbits your Greyhound may be lured farther and farther away? Deer are irresistible to Greyhounds and can lead them on a high-speed chase that may end in tragedy.
✔ Look out for cliffs, roadways, and drainage culverts.
✔ Avoid wilderness areas during hunting season. Dressing your Greyhound in a bright coursing

Many Greyhounds are just as happy chasing toys in the backyard.

Know the area in which you let your dog run.

jacket helps both you and errant hunters identify him at a distance.

✔ A Greyhound running at full speed can be a dangerous missile. Collision with a tree, fence, or even a person or another dog can be fatal. Even if your dog appears well after a collision a veterinarian should examine him for a possible collapsed lung or other injury. Greyhounds love to run toward you and veer away at the last moment; you are safest if you stand perfectly still and perhaps shout or wave your arms to warn the dog away.

✔ You should never unleash your dog in an unfenced area unless he is reliable at coming on command. If your Greyhound refuses to return, don't chase him! Run (or even drive) away from him, and he is more likely to follow. Entice him back with a pole lure, squawker, or food. No matter how angry you are when you get him back, don't punish him; just don't let him loose until he's proven he's learned to come when called.

✔ When you go into wilderness areas always have a first aid kit available, along with a means of transportation to and communication with an emergency clinic.

✔ Adjust your schedule according to weather. Early mornings are best in warm weather, but some weather is too warm for any walking or running. Swimming may help, but most Greyhounds are not enthusiastic swimmers. Simply having a lake or wading pool in which to cool off can help make summer exercise tolerable.

Weather Watch

Greyhounds can thrive in almost any climate, but certain precautions must be taken in hot or cold weather. The Greyhound coat is not a thick one, and in cold climates you will want a stylish coat or cozy sweater for your dog. The ear tips are particularly vulnerable to frost damage; a close-fitting cap or "snood" made from a cut sock or sweater sleeve will save them from freezing.

Freezing weather brings other hazards. Dogs can break through thin ice on lakes, and snow and ice can pack between the toes; coating the dog's feet with vegetable oil can help prevent this. Salt on icy sidewalks irritates paw pads and must be rinsed off.

Summer can be even more dangerous. Many dogs have died because their owners wanted to have them along on a trip to town and then left them in the car for "just a second," but when they got into the store there was a long line, and in the air-conditioned comfort of the store they lost the sense of how hot it was outside—not to mention inside a closed car.

Heatstroke also occurs as a result of another well-intentioned owner mistake: taking the dog for a romp in the summer sun. Dogs do not have sweat glands and must cool themselves through evaporation from the tongue. This system is not as effective as the human system, and dogs can become overcome by heat when their owners are scarcely affected. Greyhounds do not tolerate heat as well as other dogs of their build and coat type, and their owners must be especially careful not to let them overexert themselves in hot weather. Unless you are taking your dog for a swim, in hot weather leave him at home in the daytime and schedule your outings for early morning or evening.

TIP

Acidosis and Exertional Rhabdomyolysis

After strenuous galloping watch your dog closely for signs of *acidosis*, which can develop a few minutes to a day after exercise. Dogs that are run harder than they are in condition to run build up L-lactic acid in rapidly contracting muscles, such as those in the thighs and along the loin. The L-lactic acid causes them to swell and causes cramping, pain, and stiffness; difficulty urinating may also exist. A whirlpool bath or a massage can help sore muscles feel better.

In a more severe form, often called *acute acidosis syndrome* or *exertional rhabdomyolysis*, the dog may become so debilitated that he has difficulty walking, and is in pain even when sitting or lying down. Dogs become dehydrated and may pass dark, wine-colored urine. Without immediate veterinary treatment kidney failure and muscle loss can occur.

Both conditions can be avoided by running only a fit dog, not running too hard or too often, keeping your dog hydrated with electrolyte supplements, and feeding a balanced diet that is not too high in carbohydrates.

Walking and Jogging

Walking is excellent low-impact exercise for both of you, and is especially good for elderly or recovering dogs. Keep up a brisk pace, and gradually work up to longer distances. A healthy Greyhound should walk at least a half-mile (1.6 km) daily, and would prefer to walk several miles.

For a walk around the neighborhood, use a martingale collar that cannot slip over your Greyhound's head. Retractable leashes are great for walks, but you must be especially vigilant when using them because dogs can still dart out into the path of traffic when on them. Hold your dog close around stray animals and passing pedestrians.

Jogging can also be fun for your Greyhound, but you must work up to longer distances gradually and avoid hot weather. Heatstroke in jogging dogs has taken the lives of far too many. Check the footpads regularly for abrasions, gravel, or blistering from hot pavement. In winter, check between the pads for balls of ice and rinse the feet when returning from walking on rock salt.

Jogging your dog beside a bicycle or car can be risky, especially in cat- or squirrel-inhabited areas. If you do elect to try the lazy way out you must train your dog to understand *"Heel"* before starting, and have your dog in *heel* position—but farther out from you—when on the move.

Greyhounds are elegant additions to any home, but they are more than decorative accessories; they are finely tuned athletes awaiting their chance to push themselves to the limit and drink in the wind. Do your best to give them this chance, but as the sensible half of the partnership, don't take chances when it comes to safety.

The musculature of the Greyhound. Greyhounds have well-developed muscles that depend upon protein for fuel.

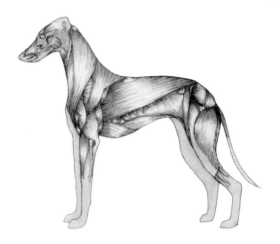

Out of the Running

Running free in the yard or park is not the same as running in competition. When free running, your dog can slow down or stop when he gets tired. Although he could also do this when in competition, he will not. He will try as hard as he possibly can as long as a lure or a hare is in sight, and he will continue to try even if he injures himself doing so. It's neither fair nor safe to place an out-of-condition Greyhound in that situation.

Not all retired racers should run competitively. Start with a complete physical examination performed by your veterinarian. Even if your dog gets a clean bill of health, don't stop there. Many racers were retired because of injuries, and running at full speed can further injure them. If you don't know why your Greyhound was retired, ask your adoption group or contact your dog's previous trainer yourself and find out the trainer's opinion. Besides injuries, some dogs may have been retired because they purposely interfered or fought with other racers while running. These dogs will probably continue this bad habit when chasing a lure, a habit that can ruin the careers of their victims. Most Greyhounds are retired simply because they were just not quite fast enough, however. These dogs may have the makings of successful coursing dogs, where speed is not the only attribute necessary for success.

Shaping Up

A retired racer may have been relatively inactive for several weeks, months, or years before coming to you. Even if they were racing recently, most racing Greyhounds run only about three times a week, and for only short sprints. Competitive amateur running is more strenuous than racing, often requiring several runs in one day, running on consecutive days of a weekend, running for longer distances than typical races, and including lots of sudden turns that require repeated braking, turning, and acceleration.

Despite your natural inclination to fatten up your skinny Greyhound, if you plan to run your dog competitively he needs to stay at fit racing weight. If you have access to your dog's racing records you can see his racing weight printed in every racing program. This weight is made up of muscle, not fat. Your dog should weigh no more than 2 or 3 pounds (.9–1.4 kg) over his racing weight.

Long walks are the best way to begin conditioning. Work up to several miles, and also allow your dog to run free in your fenced yard. After several weeks let him run free in a safe larger area. Continue to alternate days walking and running, gradually building up the free running times. Always warm up your dog with walking

Always check your Greyhound's feet for foreign objects or injuries.

and slow running before allowing him to blast off at top speed, and always give him a cool-down walk after a strenuous run. Provide plenty of water in small helpings; water with electrolytes can be especially helpful.

Note: To check your dog's hydration pick up the skin on the back just above the shoulders, so that it makes a slight tent above the body. It should "pop" back into place almost immediately. If it remains tented and separated from the body, your dog is dehydrated.

Don't let your dog run to the point of exhaustion. If he is sore following a run he should be rested and your regime should be cut back.

Lameness Therapies

A veterinarian should examine any lameness that persists without significant improvement after three days of complete rest. Ice packs may help minimize swelling if applied immediately after an injury. Cold therapy can be helpful for up to a week following an injury.

Heat therapy can be beneficial to older injuries. Heat increases the metabolic rate of the tissue, relaxes muscle spasms, and can provide some pain relief. Moist heat applied for about 20-minute periods is preferable; care must be taken to avoid burning. Other types of heat therapy are available that penetrate more deeply through the tissues, but carry a greater risk of burn injury.

Complete rest and total inactivity are the best initial home care for any lameness. Rest your dog well past the time he stops limping. Controlled exercise therapy is also important. Leash walking and swimming are excellent low-impact exercises for recovering dogs.

In many injuries in which the limb must be rested, passive motion can be important in preventing muscle contraction and maintaining the health of the joint. All movements should be slow and well within the joint's normal range of motion. Massage therapy can be useful for loosening tendons and increasing circulation.

Many injuries are quite painful and may require drug therapy for pain relief. Orthopedic surgeries can be particularly painful and almost always warrant analgesics. Pain has a self-perpetuating aspect, which means that it is easier to prevent than to stop. Discuss with your veterinarian the pros and cons of various analgesics.

Foot Injuries

✔ Burrs, cuts, peeled pads, broken nails, or other foot injuries can cause lameness.

✔ Treat split nails by trimming short and soaking in warm salt water. Apply an antibiotic and

Normal toe placement, a dropped toe (due to tearing of the superficial digital flexor tendon), and a knocked up toe (due to tearing of the deep digital flexor tendon). These tendons are located in the rear of the pastern or hock.

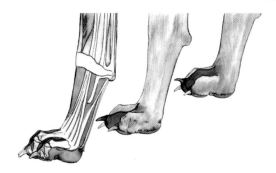

then a human fingernail mender, followed by a bandage.

✔ Flush cuts and peeled pads with warm water and cover with an antibacterial ointment and bandage.

✔ Change the dressing twice daily or anytime it gets wet. Peeled pads are very painful. A local anesthetic such as hemorrhoid cream or a topical toothache salve can help ease some pain.

Cuts: Deep cuts or extensive peeling should be checked by your veterinarian for foreign objects or tendon damage. A deep cut directly above and behind the foot may sever the ligaments to the toes, causing them to lose their arch. Immediate veterinary attention should be sought, but even that may not help.

Infections: Dogs kept in damp conditions can develop fungal and bacterial infections leading to inflammation, pain, and constant licking. The feet must be kept clean and dry. Treat painful split webbing between the toes with at least a month of inactivity; even then, it will often split again. Veterinary attention is advisable.

Toes: If a toe is swollen, does not match its fellow on the opposite foot in shape and position, makes a grinding sound when moved, or if the dog is in considerable pain, he should be kept quiet and checked by your veterinarian. Meanwhile, minimize swelling by applying cold packs or placing the foot in a bucket of cold water.

A "jammed toe" results from the stubbing of a toe on a root, rock, or other hard surface. A toe that is simply bruised will improve with rest, but any toe injury is potentially serious.

A displaced toe will stick out to the side and the dog will be in extreme pain. Pull the toe gently forward and allow it to go back into its proper position. Wrap the foot and seek veterinary attention. Toes that become dislocated often have stretched or torn ligaments, and the problem will tend to recur and worsen with each subsequent dislocation. An extended rest is mandatory. Keeping the nail of the affected toe trimmed as short as possible may help, as will wrapping the foot before running and avoiding running on hard surfaces.

One method of wrapping an injured foot is to begin near the toes with the Vet-Wrap wrapping around the leg at a 45-degree angle to the ground so that it crosses over itself and clings better.

Follow the directions outlined under the specific emergencies, call ahead to the clinic, and then transport the dog to get professional attention.

Heatstroke

Heatstroke is a serious concern in running Greyhounds. Their relatively large muscle mass and extreme exertion when running causes their body to build up high temperature in even short runs. Rapid, loud breathing, abundant thick saliva, bright red mucous membranes, and high rectal temperature are earlier signs of heatstroke. Later signs include unsteadiness, diarrhea, and coma.

Wet the dog down and place him in front of a fan.

Do not plunge the dog in ice water; the resulting constriction of peripheral blood vessels can make the situation worse. Offer small amounts of water for drinking. You must lower your dog's body temperature quickly, but do not lower it below 100°F (37.8°C). Stop cooling the dog when the temperature reaches 103°F (39.4°C).

Even after the dog seems fully recovered, do not allow him to exert himself for at least three days following the incident. Hyperthermia can cause lasting effects that can result in death unless the dog is fully recovered.

Bleeding

Consider wounds to be an emergency if there is profuse bleeding, if they are extremely deep or large, or if they open to the chest cavity, abdominal cavity, or head.

✔ If possible, elevate the wound site, and apply a cold pack to it.

✔ Do not remove impaled objects; seek veterinary attention.

✔ Cover the wound with clean dressing and apply pressure. Don't remove blood-soaked bandages; apply more dressings over them until bleeding stops.

✔ If the wound is on an extremity, apply pressure to the closest pressure point. For a front leg, press inside of the leg just above the elbow; for a rear leg, press inside of the thigh where the femoral artery crosses the thighbone; for the tail, press the underside of the tail close to where it joins the body.

✔ Use a tourniquet only in life-threatening situations and only when all other attempts have failed. Check for signs of shock.

✔ For abdominal wounds, place a warm wet sterile dressing over any protruding internal organs and cover with a bandage or towel. Do not attempt to push organs back into the dog.

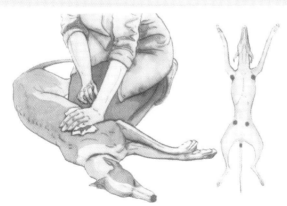

Apply pressure to the closest pressure point when dealing with uncontrolled bleeding of an extremity.

✔ For head wounds, apply gentle pressure to control bleeding. Monitor for loss of consciousness or shock and treat accordingly.

✔ For animal bites, allow some bleeding, then clean the area thoroughly and apply antibiotic ointment. A course of oral antibiotics will probably be necessary. It's best not to suture most animal bites, but a large one—over one half inch (13 mm) in diameter—or one on the face or other prominent position may need to be sutured.

Snakebite

Poisonous snakebites are characterized by swelling, discoloration, pain, fangmarks, restlessness, nausea, and weakness. Most bites are to the head, and are difficult to treat with first aid. The best first aid is to keep the dog quiet and take him to the veterinarian immediately. Antivenin is the treatment of choice.

Insect Stings and Allergic Reactions

Insects often sting dogs on the face or feet. Remove any visible stingers as quickly as possible by brushing them with a credit card or stiff paper; grasping a stinger often injects more venom into the dog. Administer a paste of baking soda and water to bee stings, and vinegar to wasp stings. A Benadryl (diphenhydramine) tablet can help thwart a local allergic reaction or itching. A dog over 50 pounds (22.7 kg) can be given up to 25 mg (one capsule) once a day.

Call your veterinarian immediately if you think the dog may be having a severe reaction. Swelling around the nose and throat can block the airway. Other reactions requiring emergency veterinary attention include restlessness, vomiting, diarrhea, seizures, and collapse.

An emergency muzzle can be fashioned from a strip of cloth or string. Follow the steps clockwise from upper left.

Fractures

Lameness associated with extreme pain, swelling or deformation of the affected leg, or grinding or popping sounds could indicate a break or another serious problem. Attempts to immobilize fractures with splints tend to do more harm than good, so it's best to keep the dog still and cushion the limb from further trauma without splinting if you can get to the veterinarian right away.

Muscle Injuries

The most common non-foot injuries are muscle injuries. These usually cause little lameness but pronounced swelling, or can be felt as an indentation in a muscle. Torn muscles may need surgery for a complete recovery. All muscle injuries should be treated with an initial ice pack followed by at least a week's rest.

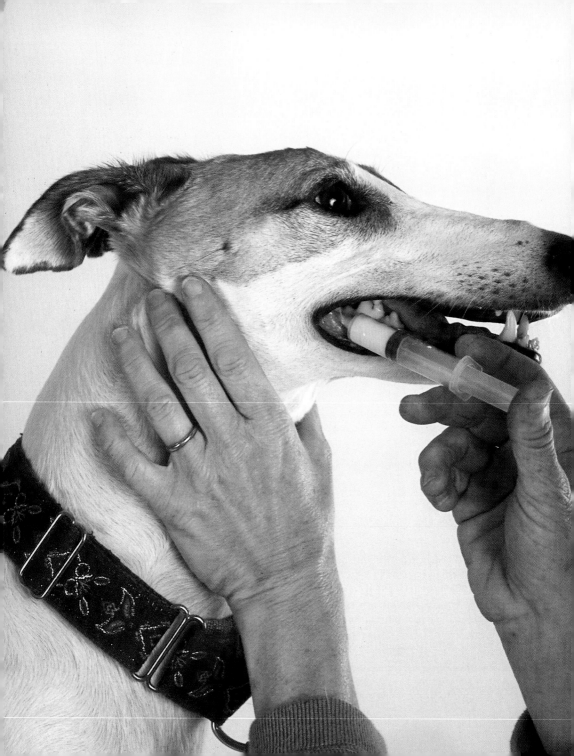

Preventive medicine encompasses accident prevention, vaccinations, parasite control, and health monitoring. Overseeing your Greyhound's good health is a team effort directed by your veterinarian but undertaken by you. Choose your veterinarian carefully, and take your duties seriously.

Greyhound Physiology Differences

Your veterinarian should be aware of several aspects of Greyhound physiology and health that may be different from the average dog. Greyhound veterinarians should be familiar with the following areas.

Anesthesia

Several years ago anesthetizing a Greyhound was somewhat risky. Today it is considerably safer, but still entails some risks.

Greyhounds do not tolerate barbiturates as readily as most other dogs. This is partly because thiobarbiturates are lipid soluble and rely on the dog's fat to be metabolized, and partly because of differences in liver function. In other words, even a fat Greyhound does not respond to thiobarbiturates as an average dog does. Greyhounds administered thiobarbiturates tend to be affected by the drug for a longer time and have an increased risk of hypothermia, hypotension, and death.

Take your medicine!

Greyhounds are also susceptible to malignant hyperthermia, in which certain drugs commonly used during anesthesia cause prolonged forceful muscle contraction, which in turn causes pronounced temperature elevation and death. Prompt cooling, intravenous fluids, and administration of Dantrolene can save the dog.

Hematology

One of the first things checked in a blood sample is the packed cell volume (PCV, also called the hematocrit), which is a measure of the percentage of red blood cells in the blood. In most dogs this averages about 35 to 55 percent, but in Greyhounds it is typically about 50 to 65 percent. Such high levels in other breeds could indicate dehydration, which is not the case in most Greyhounds.

Another important component of blood are platelets, which form blood clots to stop bleeding. Most dogs have about 200,000 to 500,000 platelets per microliter, but Greyhounds average about 150,000 per microliter. Some Greyhounds have been treated for diseases characterized by lowered platelet numbers when they were normal numbers for Greyhounds.

Tick-borne Diseases

Many Greyhounds come from kennels in which tick infestation has been a problem, and many Greyhounds subsequently develop tick-borne diseases. Some adoption groups routinely treat or test their dogs for these diseases prior to placement, but not all can afford to do so. The most common tick-borne diseases are ehrlichiosis and babesiosis.

Ehrlichiosis: *Ehrlichia canis* is a rickettsial organism transmitted from a brown tick bite. Initial signs include fever, poor appetite, nasal and ocular discharge, a tendency to bruise or bleed easily, enlarged lymph nodes, and anemia. These signs will usually disappear after a couple of weeks, but some Greyhounds will have a chronic form of the disease that emerges several months later. Signs include poor appetite, weight loss, anemia, lethargy, and bruising. Some dogs will have only some signs, and they may come and go, making diagnosis difficult.

Babesiosis: *Babesia canis* is most prevalent in the southeastern United States, where over half of all Greyhounds may be infected. Signs include anemia, fever, loss of appetite, yellowish color to the mucous membranes, and lethargy.

Dogs with tick-borne diseases often have subtle symptoms that come and go; sometimes owners say they "just don't seem quite right." Left untreated, eventually the symptoms can become profound and the dog's life endangered. Any retired racer, or any dog that has had ticks, that just doesn't seem right, or that seems unusually tired, has appetite or weight loss, fevers, or spontaneous bleeding, should have blood drawn by a veterinarian and sent to a laboratory experienced in running tick panels. They will check for antibodies to *Ehrlichia canis* (and optimally also other less common species of

Ehrlichia: E. risticii, E. equi, and *E. platys*), *Babesia,* Rocky Mountain spotted fever, and Lyme disease. The presence of antibodies in the blood indicates that the dog has been exposed to that organism but may not necessarily be currently infected; a high number of antibodies indicates a greater likelihood of an active infection. Antibiotic treatment during the initial phase is usually effective, but is less so once the disease becomes chronic.

Internal Parasites

Internal parasites can rob your dog of vital nutrients, good health, and sometimes even a long life. The most common internal parasites set up housekeeping in the heart and intestines.

Heartworms

Heartworms are deadly parasites carried by mosquitoes. Wherever mosquitoes are present, dogs should be on heartworm prevention. Several effective types of heartworm preventive are available, with some also preventing many other types of worms. Some require daily

Greyhounds as Blood Donors

Greyhounds are the most popular breed of dog for donating blood because of their cooperative nature, easily accessible blood vessels, and mostly, good and plentiful blood. About 11 percent of a fit Greyhound's body weight is made up of blood, compared to 7 percent in most other dogs. The high PCV of Greyhound blood makes it especially beneficial to most dogs needing a transfusion. Many clinics will exchange blood screening and yearly exams for your dog to act as a blood donor on call for emergencies.

administration; others require only monthly administration. The latter type is more popular and actually has a wider margin of safety and protection. They don't stay in the dog's system for a month, but instead act on a particular stage in the heartworm's development. Giving the drug each month prevents any heartworms from ever maturing. In warm areas your dog may need to be on prevention year-round, but in milder climates your dog may need to use prevention only during the warmer months. Your veterinarian can advise you.

If you forget to give the drug as prescribed, your dog may get heartworms. A dog with suspected heartworms should not be given the daily preventive because a fatal reaction could occur. The most common way of checking for heartworms is to check the blood for circulating microfilarae (the immature form of heartworms), but this method may fail to detect the presence of adult heartworms in as many as 20 percent of all tested dogs. An "occult" heartworm test is for the presence of antigens to heartworms in the blood and is more accurate. With either test, the presence of heartworms will not be detectable until nearly seven months after infection. Heartworms are treatable in their early stages, but the treatment is expensive and not without risks, although a less risky treatment has recently become available. If untreated, heartworms can kill your dog.

Intestinal Parasites

Internal parasites are common when large groups of dogs commingle, and many Greyhounds fresh out of the kennels are infested with them. Left untreated, worms can cause vomiting, diarrhea, dull coat, listlessness, and anemia. Don't be tempted to pick up some

TIP

Home Safety

Any place your Greyhound may wander must be Greyhound-proofed. The first step is to do everything you would do to baby-proof your home.

✔ Greyhounds may not understand the concept of heights, and they could leap from balconies or fall down stairs.

✔ Greyhounds can run into clear glass doors, which can be deadly at high speed. Place stickers at Greyhound eye level on all glass doors. Slamming doors, including car doors, have claimed many a Greyhound's tail. Swinging doors can catch and strangle a dog that gets partway through and then decides to try to back out. Doors leading to unfenced outdoor areas should be kept securely shut. A screen door is a vital safety feature.

✔ Check the yard for poisonous plants, bushes with sharp, broken branches at Greyhound eye level, and trees with dead branches or heavy fruits in danger of falling. Greyhounds can charge around the yard at breakneck speed, so you must remove anything that a leg or foot could hit. If you have a pool, familiarize your dog with how to get out of it should he fall in.

worm medication and worm your dog yourself; over-the-counter dewormers are largely ineffective and often more dangerous than those available through your veterinarian. Some heartworm preventives also prevent most types of intestinal worms (but not tapeworms). Protozoan parasites, such as coccidia and especially

Giardia, can cause chronic or intermittent diarrhea. Your veterinarian can diagnose them with a stool specimen and prescribe appropriate medication.

Give It Your Best Shot

Your Greyhound should receive rabies and DHLP (distemper, canine hepatitis, leptospirosis, and parvovirus) vaccinations. Vaccinations are also available for corona virus, kennel cough, and Lyme disease, but may be optional depending upon your dog's lifestyle.

Recent studies have implicated repeated vaccinations using combination vaccines with some immune system problems. Some veterinarians thus recommend staggering different types of vaccines, and vaccinating every three years instead of yearly, except where laws require more frequent rabies boosters. This is an area of current controversy and research; check with your veterinarian for the latest updates. Regardless, no dog that is under stress or not "acting

right" should be vaccinated. Many dogs seem to feel under the weather for a day or so after getting their vaccinations, so don't schedule your appointment the day before boarding, a trip, or a big doggy event.

Common Health Problems

Like people, dogs often feel under the weather. Sometimes it is not cause for alarm, but if a problem persists for more than a couple of days, it is worth getting your veterinarian's opinion. Following is an outline of the most common symptoms and some of their possible causes.

Diarrhea

Diarrhea can result from overexcitement or nervousness, a change in diet or water, sensitivity to certain foods, overeating, intestinal parasites, viral or bacterial infections, or ingestion of toxic substances. Bloody diarrhea, diarrhea with vomiting, fever, or other signs of toxicity, or diarrhea that lasts for more than a day should not be allowed to continue without veterinary advice. Some of these could be symptomatic of potentially fatal disorders.

Less severe diarrhea can be treated at home by withholding or severely restricting food and water for 24 hours. Ice cubes can be given to satisfy thirst. Administer human diarrhea medication in the same weight dosage as recommended for humans. A bland diet consisting of rice, tapioca, or cooked macaroni, along with cottage cheese or tofu for protein, should be given for several days. Feed nothing else; the intestinal tract needs time off in order to heal.

Your Greyhound's health is in your hands.

*Shield your dog from ticks and other
parasites that can carry diseases.*

Vomiting

Vomiting is a common occurrence that may or may not indicate a serious problem.

✔ Vomiting after eating grass is usually of no great concern.

✔ Vomiting immediately after meals could indicate an obstruction of the esophagus.

✔ Repeated vomiting could indicate that the dog has eaten spoiled food, undigestible objects, or may have a stomach illness. Veterinary advice should be sought. Meanwhile, withhold food, or feed as directed for diarrhea, and restrict water.

✔ Consult your veterinarian immediately if your dog vomits a foul substance resembling fecal matter, indicating a blockage in the intestinal tract, blood (partially digested blood resembles coffee grounds), or if there is projectile or continued vomiting.

✔ Sporadic vomiting with poor appetite and generally poor condition could indicate internal parasites or a more serious internal disease that should also be checked by your veterinarian.

Coughing

Any persistent cough should be checked by your veterinarian. Coughing irritates the throat and can lead to secondary infections if allowed to continue unchecked. It can also be miserable for the dog. Allergies, foreign bodies, pneumonia, parasites, tracheal collapse, tumors, and especially kennel cough and heart disease can all cause coughing.

Kennel cough: This is a highly communicable air-borne disease caused by several different infectious agents. It is characterized by a gag-ging cough appearing about a week after exposure. Inoculations are available and are an especially good idea if you plan to have your dog around other dogs at training classes or while being boarded.

Heart disease: This disease can cause coughing, most often following exercise or in the evening. Affected dogs will often lie down and point their nose in the air in order to breathe better. Drug treatment is essential.

Urinary Tract Diseases

If your dog has difficulty or pain in urination, urinates suddenly and often but in small amounts, or passes cloudy or bloody urine, she may be suffering from a problem of the bladder, urethra, or, in the case of males, prostate. Dribbling of urine during sleep can indicate a hormonal problem. Urinalysis and a rectal exam by your veterinarian are necessary to diagnose the exact nature of the problem. Bladder infections must be treated promptly to prevent the infection from reaching the kidneys.

Blockage of urine can result in death. Inability to urinate requires immediate emergency veterinary attention.

Kidney disease: Ultimately leading to kidney failure, this is one of the most common ailments of older dogs. The earliest symptom is usually increased urination. Although the excessive urination may cause problems in keeping your house clean or your night's sleep intact, never try to restrict water from a dog with kidney disease. Increased urination can also be a sign of diabetes or a urinary tract infection. Your veterinarian can discover the cause with some simple tests, and each of these conditions can be treated. For kidney disease, a low-protein and low-sodium diet can slow the progression.

In males, infections of the *prostate gland* can lead to repeated urinary tract infections, and sometimes painful defecation or blood and pus in the urine. Castration and long-term antibiotic therapy is required for improvement.

Impacted Anal Sacs

Constant licking of the anus or scooting of the anus along the ground are characteristic signs of anal sac impaction. Dogs have two anal sacs that are normally emptied by rectal pressure during defecation. Their musky-smelling contents may also be forcibly ejected when a dog is extremely frightened. Sometimes they fail to empty properly and become impacted or infected. This is more common in obese dogs, dogs with allergies or seborrhea, and dogs that seldom have firm stools. Impacted sacs cause extreme discomfort and can become infected. Treatment consists of manually emptying the sacs and administering antibiotics. As a last resort, the sacs may be removed surgically.

The Medicine Chest

✔ rectal thermometer
✔ scissors
✔ tweezers
✔ sterile gauze dressings
✔ self-adhesive bandage (such as Vet-Wrap)
✔ instant cold compress
✔ antidiarrhea medication
✔ ophthalmic ointment
✔ hand soap
✔ antiseptic skin ointment
✔ hydrogen peroxide
✔ clean sponge
✔ pen light
✔ syringe
✔ towel
✔ first aid instructions
✔ veterinarian and emergency clinic numbers; poison control center number

In Case of Emergency

Even experienced dog owners have a difficult time deciding what constitutes a true emergency; when in doubt, err on the side of caution and call the emergency clinic or your veterinarian.

1. Know the phone number and location of the emergency veterinarian in your area. Keep the number next to the phone; don't rely on your memory during an emergency.

2. Always keep enough fuel in your car to make it to the emergency clinic without stopping for gas.

3. Finally, stay calm. It will help you help your dog, and will help your dog stay calm as well. A calm dog is less likely to go into shock.

In general:

✔ Make sure you and the dog are in a safe location.

Greyhound Medical Synopsis

(Photocopy for your veterinarian)

Greyhounds have several unique physiological conditions; the following list has been prepared for easy reference.

Anesthesia Precautions
✔ Never give thiobarbiturates; they are not metabolized as quickly as in other breeds.
✔ Always provide I.V. fluids during all surgical procedures.
✔ A synthetic narcotic drug such as Oxymorphone is a good choice for preanesthesia.
✔ Isoflurane is the most commonly used anesthetic; however, Greyhounds are susceptible to malignant hyperthermia, which may be more common with inhalants. Dantrolene should be on hand.
✔ Contact the Small Animal Teaching Hospital of Colorado State University for current anesthesia protocols (303-484-9154).

Hematology
✔ PCV is higher than reported norms, averaging 50–65 percent.
✔ Hemoglobin is higher than reported norms.
✔ Platelet numbers are lower than reported norms, averaging 150,000/microliter.
✔ Greyhounds from some racing kennels have a high incidence of babesia and ehrlichia.

Cardiology
✔ Heart size is comparatively larger than in other breeds, averaging 1.2 percent of their body weight compared to 0.5 percent in other breeds.
✔ Heart sounds are amplified because of the large heart size, narrow chest, and strong beat.
✔ Left ventricular wall thickness is greater than in other breeds.

Thyroid Level
Most normal Greyhounds test in the low–normal T_4 range; unless clinical signs of hypothyroidism also exist, thyroid supplementation is probably not necessary.

Predispositions to Disorders
✔ Gastric dilatation volvulus.
✔ Pannus (superficial stromal keratitis).
✔ Osteosarcoma.
✔ Pemphigus.
✔ Tail tip trauma; conservative treatment with lightweight bandage is best; use a lightweight hollow curler for protection, if needed.

Common Features of Ex-Racers
Bald thigh syndrome: Not usually responsive to thyroid supplementation.

Clitoral hypertrophy: A reddened, polyplike area on the vulva; common result of testosterone administration when racing; no treatment is needed.

Old injuries: Most common racing injuries are fibular, carpal, metacarpal, tarsal, and toe fractures; torn gastronemius, triceps, gracilis, biceps femoris, sartorius, rectus femoris, and lateral vastus muscles; torn plantar and collateral toe ligaments; torn Achilles and flexor carpi ulnaris muscle tendons; and shoulder, carpal, lumbosacral, stifle, hock, and toe joint injuries.

Alabama rot (idiopathic cutaneous and renal glomerular vasculopathy): Rare in Greyhounds once off the track; usually begins on the lower rear extremities with rapidly ulcerating and spreading skin lesions, followed by fever, swelling, diarrhea, vomiting, and finally acute kidney failure and death within 24 hours. Researchers at Kansas State University have implicated *E. coli* infection from 4D meat.

Lungworm: Greyhounds have the highest incidence (although still low) of lungworms of any breed.

Suggested Reading
International Greyhound Research Database: *http://www.agcouncil.com/*

Blythe, L., Gannon, R., and Craig, A. *Care of the Racing Greyhound.* Abilene, Kansas: American Greyhound Council, 1994.

Bloomberg, M., Dee, J., and Taylor, R. *Canine Sports Medicine and Surgery.* Philadelphia, Pennsylvania: W.B. Saunders, 1998.

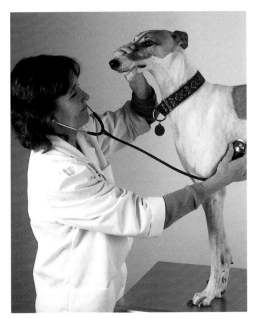

Regular veterinarian examinations help diagnose and treat common health problems.

Tale of the Tail

Greyhounds have whiplike tails that are easily injured from exuberant wagging. Most commonly, the tip of the tail is abraded from hitting walls or furniture. Apply antibiotic ointment and place the tip inside a lightweight mesh hair curler for protection without compromising air circulation. You can also tie the tail to the hind leg to prevent it from wagging but you must remember to untie it when the dog relieves herself. In some cases the tail may be broken. A simple Popsicle stick splint held on with tape has a greater chance of success than a heavy bandage, which too often leads to loss of blood supply. Amputation may be necessary in either case.

✔ Make sure breathing passages are open. Remove any collar and check the mouth and throat.
✔ Move the dog as little and as gently as possible.
✔ Control any bleeding.
✔ Check breathing, pulse, and consciousness.
✔ Check for signs of shock: very pale gums, weakness, unresponsiveness, faint pulse, shivering. Treat by keeping the dog warm and calm.
✔ Never use force or do anything that causes extreme discomfort.
✔ Never remove an impaled object, unless it is blocking the airway.

Bloat (Gastric Torsion, Gastric Dilatation-Volvulus)

Bloat is a life-threatening emergency in which gas and fluid become trapped in the stomach. Symptoms include distention of the abdomen, unproductive attempts to vomit, excessive salivation, and restlessness. A dog with these symptoms needs to be taken to the emergency clinic right now—not tomorrow, not even an hour from now. No home treatment is possible.

The veterinarian will try to pass a tube into the stomach so gases can escape. Often the stomach has twisted and rotated on its axis, though, so the tube can't get into the stomach. These dogs require emergency surgery in order to save their lives. The rotation of the stomach cuts off the blood supply to the cells of the stomach wall, which will die and subsequently kill the dog if surgery isn't performed quickly. Other organs may also be compromised. During surgery the veterinarian should tack the stomach in place to prevent future rotation. Dogs that bloat once will often continue to do so without this tacking procedure (see page 34 for tips on avoiding bloat).

Even the most careful owners and cautious dogs can have accidents. Be prepared.

Poisoning

Symptoms and treatment vary depending upon the specific poison. In most cases, home treatment is not advisable. If in doubt about whether poison was ingested, call the veterinarian anyway. If possible, bring the poison and its container with you to the veterinarian.

Two of the most common and life-threatening poisons eaten by dogs are Warfarin (rodent poison) and especially ethylene glycol (antifreeze). Veterinary treatment must be obtained within two to four hours of ingestion

of even tiny amounts if the dog's life is to be saved. *Do not wait for symptoms.*

Signs of poisoning vary according to the type of poison, but commonly include vomiting, convulsions, staggering, and collapse.

Call the veterinarian or poison control hotline and give as much information as possible. Induce vomiting—except in the cases outlined below—by giving either hydrogen peroxide (mixed 1:1 with water), salt water, or dry mustard and water. Treat for shock and get the dog to the veterinarian at once. Be prepared for convulsions or respiratory distress.

Do not induce vomiting if the poison was an acid, alkali, petroleum product, solvent, cleaner, tranquilizer, or if a sharp object was swallowed; also do not induce vomiting if the dog is severely depressed, convulsing, comatose, or if over two hours have passed since ingestion. If the dog is not convulsing or unconscious: Dilute the poison by giving milk, vegetable oil, or egg whites. Activated charcoal can adsorb many toxins. Baking soda or milk of magnesia can be given for ingested acids, and vinegar or lemon juice for ingested alkalis.

Osteosarcoma

Large, long-legged dogs tend to be more prone to oesteosarcoma (bone cancer), and unfortunately, Greyhounds are no exception. Although it can occur anywhere, it most often appears on the long bones of the front legs. The most typical sign is lameness that does not improve with rest. A radiograph can provide a fairly conclusive diagnosis. The condition is very painful and the only way to alleviate the pain is by amputating the limb. Studies in humans have shown that amputating a painful limb often results in lingering phantom limb pain, but that by numbing the limb for a period of time (often a day or more) before amputation, the chance of phantom limb pain is greatly reduced. Ask your veterinarian to consider this option for your dog. Most Greyhounds learn to cope well with life on three legs, and can usually walk within a week. Unfortunately, even with aggressive treatment, survival time may only be a matter of months.

The only way you will know if your Greyhound may be sick is to become intimately in tune with him when he's well. Take five minutes weekly to perform a simple health check on your Greyhound, examining
• the mouth for red, bleeding, swollen, or pale gums, loose teeth, ulcers of the tongue or gums, or bad breath.
• the eyes for discharge, cloudiness, or discolored "whites."
• the ears for foul odor, redness, discharge, or crusted tips.
• the nose for thickened or colored discharge.
• the skin for parasites, hair loss, crusts, red spots, or lumps.

• the feet for cuts, abrasions, split nails, bumps, or misaligned toes.
✔ Observe your dog for signs of lameness or incoordination, sore neck, circling, loss of muscling, and for any behavioral change.
✔ Run your hands over the muscles and bones and check that they are symmetrical from one side to the other.
✔ Weigh your dog and observe whether she is putting on fat or wasting away.
✔ Check for any growths or swellings, which could indicate cancer or a number of less serious problems.

✔ Check for sores that don't heal or any pigmented lump that begins to grow or bleed.
✔ Look out for mammary masses, changes in testicle size, discharge from the vulva or penis, increased or decreased urination, foul-smelling or strangely colored urine, incontinence, swollen abdomen, black or bloody stool, change in appetite or water consumption, difficulty breathing, lethargy, gagging, or loss of balance.

Temperature and Pulse

To take your dog's temperature, lubricate a rectal thermometer (preferably the digital type), insert it about 2 inches (5 cm) into the dog's anus, and leave it for about one minute. Normal temperature for a Greyhound is around 101°F (38°C), ranging from 100 to 102.5°F (37.8–39°C). Call your veterinarian if the temperature is over 104°F (40°C).

A good place to check the pulse is on the femoral artery, located inside the rear leg, where the thigh meets the abdomen. Normal pulse rates range from 80 to 140 beats per minute in an awake Greyhound, and are strong and fairly regular.

In the following home health exam, any "yes" answers require a veterinary examination.

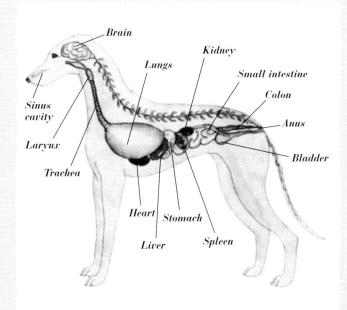

The internal organs of the Greyhound.

HOME HEALTH CHECK

Make several copies of this chart and keep a record of your dog's home exams.

Date: _____Temperature: _____ Pulse: _____

First consider your dog's general behavior. Is your dog:

____ Restless?
____ Tired?
____ Irritable?
____ Weak?
____ Confused?
____ Limping?
____ Acting dizzy?
____ Bumping into things?
____ Eating a lot less than usual?
____ Eating a lot more than usual?
____ Drinking a lot more than usual?
____ Urinating a lot more than usual?
____ Having difficulty urinating?
____ Having accidents in the house?
____ Having diarrhea?
____ Vomiting or trying to vomit?
____ Coughing?
____ Breathing more rapidly than usual?

Now give your dog's body a more thorough exam.

Check the nose for:
____ Thick or colored discharge
____ Sudden loss of color
____ Sores or crustiness

Check the mouth for:
____ Bad breath
____ Soreness
____ Loose teeth
____ Dirty teeth
____ Gum color: ____ pink (good)
    ____ almost white ____ bright red
    ____ yellowish ____ bluish
    ____ red spots (anything but pink requires a veterinary exam)
____ Swollen gums
____ Bleeding
____ Sores
____ Growths

Check the eyes for:
____ Watery tears
____ Thick discharge
____ Squinting
____ Pawing at an eye
____ Swollen eye
____ Cloudy or dull surface
____ Red sclera ("whites")
____ Unequal sized pupils

Check the ears for:
____ Bad smell
____ Redness inside
____ Lots of black ear wax
____ Scabby ear tips
____ Head shaking
____ Head carried tilted
____ Ear scratching
____ Painfulness

Check the feet for:
____ Cuts
____ Split nails
____ Long nails
____ Swollen toes
____ Toes out of alignment

Check the skin for:
____ Parasites
____ Black "flea dirt"
____ Hair loss
____ Scabs
____ Red spots
____ Lumps
____ Sores

Check the anal and genital regions for:
____ Swelling
____ Redness
____ Discharge
____ Dog constantly licking at its anus
____ Dog scooting rear end on ground
____ Black or bloody stool
____ Bloody urine
____ Signs of diarrhea

You and your Greyhound have a lifetime of experiences to share. Your life may change in the years to come, but for better or worse, your Greyhound will still love and depend on you. Always remember the promise you made before you made the commitment to share your life: to love and care for him every day of his life with as much enthusiasm as you did the first day he arrived home.

The Greyhound's natural athleticism sometimes misleads owners into forgetting that Greyhounds, like all dogs, get old. One day you will look at your youngster and be shocked to discover that his face has silvered and his gait has stiffened. He sleeps longer and more soundly than he used to, and is slower to get going. He is less eager to play and more content to lie in the sun. Yet the older Greyhound, his eyes often hazy from cataracts, his gait stiff, and his face gray, is, in the opinion of many Greyhound lovers, the most beautiful Greyhound of all.

Senior Diets

Both physical activity and metabolic rates decrease in older animals, so they require fewer calories to maintain their weight. Feeding old dogs the same as young dogs makes fat dogs. Fat dogs have a greater risk of cardiovascular and joint problems.

Although some geriatric dogs are overweight, other Greyhounds lose weight and may need to

Greyhounds age gracefully.

eat a high-calorie food in order to keep the pounds on. Most senior Greyhounds do not require a special diet unless they have a particular medical need for it.

Older dogs should be fed several small meals instead of one large meal, and should be fed on time. Moistening dry food or feeding canned food can help a dog with dental problems enjoy his meal.

Old Dogs, New Tricks

It's important to keep your dog active, but exercise should be moderated. Walking or swimming is easier on old joints than running. Mental stimulation is also important. Teaching your old dog a new trick every month is a good way to keep his mind young.

Older dogs may experience hearing or visual loss. Be careful not to startle a dog with impaired senses, as a startled dog could snap in self-defense. The slight haziness that appears in the older dog's pupils is normal and has minimal effect upon vision, but some dogs, especially those with diabetes, may develop cataracts. These can be removed by a veterinary ophthalmologist if they are severe. Dogs with gradual vision loss can cope well as long as they are kept in familiar surroundings and extra safety precautions are followed. Some older dogs become cranky and less patient, especially when dealing with puppies or boisterous children. But don't just excuse behavioral changes, especially if they are sudden, as due simply to aging. They could be symptoms of pain or disease.

Long trips may be grueling, and boarding in a kennel may be upsetting. The immune system may be less effective in older dogs, so that it is increasingly important to shield your dog from infectious disease, chilling, overheating, and any stressful conditions.

Arthritis

While Greyhounds of any age enjoy a soft warm bed, it is an absolute necessity for older Greyhounds. Degenerative joint disease (DJD), more commonly called arthritis, is a common cause of intermittent stiffness and lameness. In some older dogs there is no obvious cause. In others, abnormal stresses or trauma to the joint can cause degeneration of the joint cartilage and underlying bone. The synovial membrane surrounding the joint becomes inflamed and the bone develops small bony outgrowths called *osteophytes*. These changes cause the joint to stiffen, become painful, and have decreased range of motion. In cases in which an existing condition is exacerbating the DJD, surgery to remedy the condition is warranted.

When considering surgery for a joint problem, keep in mind that the more the joint is used in its damaged state, the more DJD will occur. Even though surgery may solve the initial problem, if too much damage has taken place, the dog will still be plagued with incurable arthritic changes. Prevention of arthritis is the key.

Conservative treatment entails keeping the dog's weight down, attending to injuries, and maintaining a program of exercise. Low-impact exercise such as walking or swimming every other day is best for dogs with signs of arthritis. Newer drugs, such as carprofen, are available from your veterinarian and may help alleviate some of the symptoms of DJD, but they should be used only with careful veterinary supervision. Some newer drugs and supplements may actually improve the joint. Polysulfated glycosaminoglycan increases the compressive resilience of cartilage. Glucosamine stimulates the synthesis of collagen, and may help rejuvenate cartilage to some extent. Chondroitin sulfate helps to shield cartilage from destructive enzymes.

Geriatric Medicine

The older dog should be seen by his veterinarian at least twice a year. Blood tests can detect early stages of diseases that can benefit from treatment. Although older dogs present a somewhat greater anesthesia risk, most of this increased risk can be negated by first performing a complete medical workup to screen for problems.

Older dogs tend to have a stronger body odor, but don't ignore increased odors. They could indicate specific problems, such as periodontal disease, impacted anal sacs, seborrhea, ear infections, or even kidney disease. Any strong odor should be checked by your veterinarian. As with people, dogs lose skin moisture as they age, and though dogs don't have to worry about wrinkles, their skin can become dry and itchy. Regular brushing can help by stimulating oil production.

Some of the more common symptoms and their possible cause in older Greyhounds include
✔ diarrhea: kidney or liver disease, pancreatitis
✔ coughing: heart disease, lung cancer
✔ difficulty eating: periodontal disease, oral tumors
✔ decreased appetite: kidney, liver, or heart disease, pancreatitis, cancer
✔ increased appetite: diabetes, hyperadrenocorticism
✔ weight loss: heart, liver, or kidney disease, diabetes, cancer
✔ abdominal distention (gradual): heart or kidney disease, hyperadrenocorticism, tumor
✔ increased urination: diabetes, kidney or liver disease, cystitis, hyperadrenocorticism
✔ limping: arthritis, cancer
✔ nasal discharge: tumor, periodontal disease

If you are lucky enough to have an old Greyhound, you still must accept that the time will come when some disease will strike. Heart disease, kidney failure, or cancer eventually claim most of these senior citizens. Early detection can help delay their effects but unfortunately can seldom prevent them ultimately.

The Friend of a Lifetime

Despite the best of care, eventually neither you nor your veterinarian can prevent your cherished friend from succumbing to old age or an incurable illness. It seems hard to believe that you will have to say good-bye to a dog that has been such a focal point of your life—in truth, a real member of your family.

Euthanasia is a difficult and personal decision that no one wants to make. Consider whether your dog has a reasonable chance of getting better, and how he seems to feel. Ask yourself if your dog is getting pleasure out of life, and if he enjoys most of his days. Financial considerations can be a factor if it means going into debt in exchange for just a little while longer. Your own emotional state must also be considered.

We all wish that if our dog has to go, he would fall asleep and never wake up. This, unfortunately, seldom happens. Even when it does, you are left with the regret that you never got to say good-bye. The closest you can come to this is with euthanasia. Euthanasia is painless and involves giving an overdose of an anesthetic. Essentially, the dog will fall asleep and die almost instantly.

Eternally in Your Heart

Many people who regarded their Greyhound as a member of the family nonetheless feel embarrassed at the grief they feel at his loss, yet this dog has often functioned as a surrogate child, best friend, and confidant. Because people are often closer to their pets than they are to distant family members, it is not uncommon to feel more grief at the loss of the pet. Unfortunately, the support from friends that comes with human loss is too often absent with pet loss. Such well-meaning but ill-informed statements as "he was just a dog" or "just get another one" do little to ease the pain, but the truth is that many people simply don't know how to react and probably aren't really as callous as they might sound. There are, however, many people who share your feelings and there are pet bereavement counselors available at many veterinary schools.

INFORMATION

Organizations

American Kennel Club
51 Madison Avenue
New York, NY 10038
(212) 696-8200
www.akc.org

AKC Registration and Information
5580 Centerview Drive, Suite 200
Raleigh, NC 27606-3390
(919) 233-9767

Greyhound Club of America (AKC)
B. A. Gordon
P.O. Box 850
La Luz, NM 88337
www.greyhoundclubofamerica.org

National Greyhound Association
P.O. Box 543
Abilene, KS 67410
(785) 263-4660
nga.jc.net

American Sighthound Field Association
c/o P.O. Box 399
Alpaugh, CA 93201
www.asfa.org

The Greyhound Project, Inc.
P.O. Box 358
Marblehead, MA 01945-0358
www.adopt-a-greyhound.org

Greyhound Pets of America
1-800-366-1472
www.greyhoundpets.org

Home Again Microchip System
1-800-LONELY ONE

Therapy Dogs International
88 Bartley Road
Flanders, NJ 07836
(973) 252-9800
www.tdi-dog.org

Magazines

Celebrating Greyhounds: The Magazine
P.O. Box 358
Marblehead, MA 01945-0358
www.adopt-a-greyhound.org

Dog World
29 North Dearborn, Suite 1100
Chicago, IL 60610
(312) 396-3600
www.dogworld-mag.com

Dog Fancy
P.O. Box 53264
Boulder, CO 80322-3264
(303) 666-8504
http://www.animalnetwork.com/dogs/

Dogs USA Annual
P.O. Box 55811
Boulder, CO 80322-5811
(303) 786-7652

The Sighthound Review
(AKC oriented)
10177 Blue River Hills Road
Manhattan, KS 66503
(785) 485-2992
www.sighthoundreview.com

The Greyhound Review
(Official publication of the NGA)
See NGA address under *Organizations*.

AKC Gazette
(Official publication of the AKC)
See AKC New York address under *Organizations*.

Field Advisory News
(Official publication of the ASFA)
See ASFA address under *Organizations*.

Books

Ash, Edward C. *The Book of the Greyhound*. London, England: Hutchinson & Co., 1933.

Barnes, Julia. *The Complete Book of Greyhounds*. New York: Howell Book House, Inc., 1994.

Blythe, Linda L., Gannon, James R., & Craig, A. Morrie. *Care of the Racing Greyhound: A Guide for Trainers, Breeders, and Veterinarians*. American Greyhound Council, 1994.

Branigan, Cynthia. *Adopting the Racing Greyhound*. New York: Howell Book House, Inc., 1992.

Burnham, Patricia G. *Playtraining Your Dog*. New York: St. Martin Press, 1980.

Coile, D. Caroline. *Barron's Encyclopedia of Dog Breeds*. Hauppauge, New York: Barron's Educational Series, Inc., 1998.

____. *Show Me! A Dog Showing Primer*. Hauppauge, New York: Barron's Educational Series, Inc., 1997.

Edwards, Clark H. *The Greyhound*. London, England: Popular Dogs Publishing Co Ltd., 1973.

Genders, Roy. *The Encyclopaedia of Greyhound Racing. A Complete History of the Sport*. London, England: Pelham Books, 1981.

Hutchinson, William. *Hutchinson on Sighthounds*. (Reprint of the sighthound sections of *Hutchinson's Dog Encyclopedia*, originally published 1934). Wheat Ridge, Colorado: Hoflin Publishing, 1976.

Kohnke, J. *Veterinary Advice for Greyhound Owners*. Hertfordshire, England: Ring Press Books Ltd., 1994.

Lackey, Sue. *Greyhounds in America, Vol. 1*. Greyhound Club of America, 1988.

LeMieux, Sue. *The Book of the Greyhound*. Neptune, New Jersey: tfh Publications, 1999.

Livingood, Lee. *Retired Racing Greyhounds for Dummies*. Foster City, California: IDG, 2000.

Miller, Constance O. *Gazehounds: The Search for Truth*. Wheat Ridge, Colorado: Hoflin Publishing, 1988. (History of all sighthounds).

Rolins, A. *All About the Greyhound*. Willoughby, NSW 2068, Australia: Rigby Publishers, 1982.

Sullivan, Mark. *The Ultimate Greyhound*. New York: Howell Book House, 1999.

Video

Greyhound #VVT411
The American Kennel Club
Attn: Video Fulfillment
5580 Centerview Drive #200
Raleigh, NC 27606
(919) 233-9780

Soundness Examination of the Racing Greyhound
James C. Gannon
available from the NGA
P.O. Box 543
Abilene, KS 67410
(785) 263-4660

I N D E X

About the Author

D. Caroline Coile, Ph.D., has owned, trained, studied, and competed with sighthounds for most of her life, and still finds them fascinating, frustrating, and fun. She has shared her findings in over 100 scientific journal and dog magazine articles, and in 19 books about dogs, including *Barron's Encyclopedia of Dog Breeds* and *Show Me! A Dog Showing Primer*. Her dog writing awards include the Dog Writer's Association of America Maxwell Award, Denlinger Award, and the Eukanuba Canine Health Award.

Her own dogs include Best in Show, Best in Specialty Show, Best in Field, and Pedigree Award winners, as well as a #1-ranked obedience Saluki. Others have never set foot in any ring but are still Best in Yard winners and #1 in various vital categories including gnawing arms off chairs, pushing people out of beds, and grabbing food off counters. This book is dedicated to them: Baha, Kara, Khyber, Bobby, Khyzi, Junior, Jeepers, Sissy, Dixie, Hypatia, Savannah, Kitty, Beany, Wolfman, Stinky, Oman, Minka, Isis, Tundra, Luna, and Honey.

Important Note

This pet owner's guide tells the reader how to buy or adopt, and care for, a Greyhound. The author and the publisher consider it important to point out that the advice given in the book is meant primarily for normally developed dogs of excellent physical health and good character.

Anyone who adopts a fully-grown dog should be aware that the animal has already formed its basic impressions of human beings. The new owner should watch the animal carefully, including its behavior toward humans.

If the dog comes from a shelter, it may be possible to get some information on the dog's background and peculiarities there. There are dogs that, as the result of bad experiences with humans, behave in an unnatural manner or may even bite. Only people that have experience with dogs should take in such animals.

Caution is further advised in the association of children with dogs, in meeting other dogs, and in exercising the dog without a leash.

Even well-behaved and carefully supervised dogs sometimes do damage to someone else's property or cause accidents. It is therefore in the owner's interest to be adequately insured against such eventualities, and we strongly urge all dog owners to purchase a liability policy that covers their dog.

Acknowledgments

The AKC Greyhound standard is reprinted courtesy of the Greyhound Club of America.

Photo Credits

Pets By Paulette: pages 2-3, 13, 16 top, 21, 33 top left, 37, 40 top right, 60 top left; Tara Darling: pages 4, 8, 17 bottom right, 25 bottom, 36, 44 bottom left, 53 bottom left, 85, 88; Close Encounters of the Furry Kind: pages 5, 12, 16 bottom left, 17 bottom left, 24 left, 24 right, 25 top, 32 middle, 32 bottom, 33 top right, 44 top, 45 top right, 45 bottom, 48, 50 bottom left, 52 top left, 52 bottom, 53 top, 56, 60 top right, 61 top left, 64, 65, 68, 72, 77, 80, 93; Kent and Donna Dannen: pages 9 bottom, 16 middle left, 32 top right, 33 bottom, 41 bottom, 44 bottom right, 53 bottom right, 57, 60 bottom right, 61 top right, 61 bottom left, 61 bottom right, 69, 81; Dale Jackson: pages 9 top, 17 top left, 40 bottom left, 89; C. W. McKeen: pages 16 middle right, 49, 52 top right; Susan Scroggins: page 16 bottom right; B. Babicki: page 17 top right; Norvia Behling: pages 20, 28, 29, 32 top left, 40 top left, 40 bottom right, 41 top, 76, 84; Joan Balzarini: 45 top left.

Cover Credits

All covers by Pets By Paulette.

All inquiries should be addressed to:
Barron's Educational Series, Inc.
250 Wireless Boulevard
Hauppauge, New York 11788
http://www.barronseduc.com
ISBN-13: 978-0-7641-1836-4
ISBN-10: 0-7641-1836-6
Library of Congress Catalog Card No. 00-068016

Library of Congress Cataloging-in-Publication Data
Coile, D. Caroline.
    Greyhounds / D. Caroline Coile.—2nd ed.
        p.   cm. — (A complete pet owner's manual)
    Includes bibliographical references (p.   ).
    ISBN 0-7641-1836-6
    1. Greyhounds. I. Title. II. Series.
SF429.G8 C635   2001
636.753'4—dc21   00-068016

Printed in China
9 8 7